Peace!

Sidney Ins.

THE BOMB

Demonstration of students in Madison, Wisconsin, protesting the planned construction of a nuclear power plant   BULLETIN OF THE ATOMIC SCIENTISTS

THE BOMB

SIDNEY LENS

ILLUSTRATED WITH PHOTOGRAPHS

LODESTAR BOOKS
E. P. Dutton   New York

I would like to thank Bob Aldridge and Dr. Michio Kaku for reading the manuscript and offering suggestions for improvement.

Copyright © 1982 by Sidney Lens

Library of Congress Cataloging in Publication Data

Lens, Sidney.
  The bomb.

  Bibliography: p.
  Includes index.
  Summary: Details the race between the U.S. and the Soviet Union for superiority in atomic weaponry since the inception of the Manhattan Project in 1939, and analyzes the danger of unleashing phenomenally destructive weapons upon the world.
    1. Atomic warfare—Juvenile literature.   2. Atomic weapons—Juvenile literature. 3.World politics—1945—Juvenile literature. [1. Atomic warfare. 2. Atomic weapons. 3.World politics—1945] I. Title.
  UF767.L395 1982   355'.0217   82-9922
  ISBN 0-525-66752-0   AACR2

Published in the United States by E. P. Dutton, Inc., 2 Park Avenue, New York, N.Y. 10016. Published simultaneously in Canada by Clarke, Irwin & Company Limited, Toronto and Vancouver.
Editor: Virginia Buckley   Designer: Trish Parcell
Printed in the U.S.A.   First edition
10 9 8 7 6 5 4 3 2 1

CONTENTS

Photographs appear after pages 3 and 61.

1. AN APOCRYPHAL STORY

"THERE IS NO ROAD TO PEACE. PEACE IS THE ROAD."
A.J. Muste, pacifist leader

Someone—we don't know who—made up this story about Jupiter, the largest planet in the solar system. Scientists on Earth, it seems, have confirmed that most of the satellites revolving around Jupiter were placed there by Nature; but two of them could not have been. Their trajectories, speed, and distance from the mother body are such that, according to Earth scientists, they must have been launched in orbit by intelligent beings. Not human beings, of course, because it is not likely that the process of evolution would have gone through the same cycle on this distant planet as on the planet Earth. But they must have been "beings" who understood the laws of thermodynamics, the theory of relativity, the intricacies of mathematics.

Since it seems certain there is no life on Jupiter today, the Earth scientists feel that some catastrophic event must have taken place there millions of years ago. Let's suppose, they say, there *was* life on Jupiter at that time; let's suppose the process of evolution brought forth a being as intelligent, as competent,

1

as technologically adept as human beings on Earth are today
—or more so. And let's suppose further that in the course of
time these intelligent beings grouped themselves into quarrel-
ing nations, just like Earthlings today, and waged war against
one another every ten or twenty years.

And let's suppose still further that in due course the two
"greatest" nations among them discovered the secrets of nuclear fission and nuclear fusion. They built atom bombs like the
one that destroyed Hiroshima here on Earth in 1945, then
hydrogen bombs a thousand times more powerful. Their leaders probably pledged on their honor that they would never use
those terrible weapons—unless the other side used them first.
But as so often happens with the best-laid plans, that pledge
was broken, and a nuclear war did break out.

No one knows how it started. It could have been by accident
—because of a malfunction in the radar system, for instance,
which falsely indicated that the other side had launched a nuclear attack; maybe the fatal button was pushed by a crazed
general who had a grudge; or perhaps it all began with a squab-
ble between two small nations that had secretly acquired nuclear weapons, and the fighting kept escalating until it got out
of hand. No matter—the end result was that billions of lives on
Jupiter were wiped out by blast and fire almost immediately,
billions more died later from radiation, and the hundreds of
millions that remained starved to death because there was no
way to grow food on irradiated land.

Those who survived for a few weeks eventually came to envy
the dead. When they emerged from their shelters they were
confronted by an unspeakable horror. Billions of cadavers
were waiting to be buried. Feasting on the rotting flesh were
trillions of mice (mice are more immune to radiation than
higher organisms). Feasting on the mice were trillions of trillions of roaches (roaches are more immune to radiation than

mice). And feasting on the roaches were an incalculable number of amoeba, who are more immune to radiation than roaches, mice, or the higher living beings.

There were also fires, and mudslides, and caved-in roads, and bridges swept away, and floods everywhere. Those who survived experienced terrible headaches as their swollen brains were pressed against their skulls. The fillings of their teeth became irradiated, and holes appeared in their tongues and inner organs. They suffered simultaneously from bloody diarrhea and vomiting; their hair fell out. Few survived for more than three weeks. In time even the mice, roaches, birds, reptiles, mammals—even the amoeba—passed away. The delicate ecological balance between living things and nature had been destroyed: Jupiter could no longer support organic beings in any form.

All that remained of past life on this massive planet, therefore, were the two lonely satellites revolving into eternity. At least that is what we are told in our apocryphal—mythical—story.

It makes one wonder: Is this to be the fate of our beautiful planet Earth too? Will nations and people continue to build great stockpiles of nuclear weapons, and will the day finally come when they use them in war, wiping out all life? And will the only evidence that you and I were once here be a single United States Mercury satellite and a single Soviet Sputnik revolving around our dead planet forever?

It makes one wonder.

Albert Einstein and Leo Szilard

Drawing of the nuclear reactor at Stagg Field, University of Chicago, where a group of scientists achieved the first self-sustaining chain reaction on December 2, 1942

Left: Robert Oppenheimer and Major W. A. Stevens on a trip to select a site for the first atomic bomb test in May 1944
BULLETIN OF THE ATOMIC SCIENTISTS

Below: Jumbo, or "Fat Man," on a flatcar in April 1945, in preparation for the nuclear explosion at Alamogordo, New Mexico LOS ALAMOS NATIONAL LABORATORY

Top: Jumbo after the nuclear blast at Alamogordo, New Mexico, on July 16, 1945

Bottom: Damage to machine tools in steel-frame building 0.6 mile from ground zero after the bombing of Hiroshima

Top: Nuclear weapon of the "Little Boy" type detonated over Hiroshima in 1945

BULLETIN OF THE ATOMIC SCIENTISTS

Bottom: Mushroom cloud after atomic bombing of Nagasaki in August 1945   UNITED NATIONS

Top: Underwater explosion on Bikini Island, July 25, 1946   U.S. NAVY

Bottom: Mushroom cloud following detonation of a hydrogen bomb in the Marshall Islands in November 1952. The test island, Elugelab, completely disappeared.   UNITED NATIONS

Titan II, a silo-launched intercontinental ballistic missile that uses storable liquid fuel

Firing of Polaris missile *(left),* which is fifty times more powerful than the Hiroshima bomb, and Poseidon missile *(right),* which carries up to fourteen warheads   U.S. NAVY

An A-3 Polaris missile being loaded on a submarine   U.S. NAVY

Top: Multi-Purpose Food was manufactured in the early 1960's for use in fallout shelters in case of nuclear attack.　　GENERAL MILLS, INC.

Bottom: Illustration of man building a fallout shelter, from a 1962 booklet distributed by the United States government　　DEPARTMENT OF DEFENSE

2. "BRIGHTER THAN A THOUSAND SUNS"

"WAR HAS BECOME NOT JUST TRAGIC BUT PREPOSTEROUS. WITH MODERN WEAPONS THERE CAN BE NO VICTORY FOR ANYONE."
General Dwight D. Eisenhower

On May 31, 1945, sixteen men met in the office of Secretary of War Henry L. Stimson. Eight of them were members of a group called the Interim Committee; four were top scientists; two were generals, including General George C. Marshall; the remaining two were associates of Stimson. The sixteen were there to make decisions about a weapon the average American had never heard of—the atom bomb. In due course they picked four future targets for "The Bomb"—Kokura, Hiroshima, Nagasaki, Niigata. The criterion in each case was that the city to be destroyed had a "war plant surrounded by workers' homes." There would be no prior warning, Stimson and his colleagues decided.

This was what might be called the "practical" part of the agenda. But the supersecret group also discussed the future. What were the chances of producing nuclear weapons more powerful than the one now being developed? How long would it take other nations, especially the Soviet Union, to catch up with the United States? What hope was there to use atomic energy for peaceful purposes, such as electricity? Everyone present was aware that something earth-shaking was being discussed—no one more so than Secretary Stimson.

They were not talking about just another weapon, Stimson told the Committee—like a new airplane or a tank. What they were discussing was "a new relationship of man to the universe." Atomic energy was a discovery, he said, comparable "to the discoveries of the Copernican theory and of the laws of gravity, but far more important than these in its effects on the lives of men." Stimson hoped that atomic energy could be controlled so as to ensure "future peace," but he also recognized that it could become "a menace to civilization" itself.

Humankind, the Secretary seemed to be saying, was at the most critical turning point in its entire recorded history. In the decades to come there would be an ongoing dispute between those who felt, like Stimson, that the atom was destined to bring about a fundamental change in the relationships between nations and people and those who felt that the bomb was merely another weapon.

How did the human species get to this juncture?

It all started rather innocently almost half a century before, in 1896, when Antoine Henri Becquerel discovered radioactivity in uranium. A radioactive element emits radiant energy in the form of alpha, beta, or gamma rays. Becquerel, of course, did not envision the atom bomb when he made his discovery. Far from it. He, together with scientists in a dozen other nations, was pursuing basic research into such interesting matters as atoms, molecules, nuclei, mass, energy. He and his colleagues were trying to shed light on the secret workings of nature, not to find new means of killing people. But as so often happens, scientific discovery is turned to purposes quite different from those intended.

The next step toward the atom bomb came in 1902, when Marie and Pierre Curie isolated a radioactive metal called radium. They were following Becquerel's discovery—investigating the uranium in pitchblende—when they found another radioactive element. After long, tedious work, they were able to separate one *gram* of radium salts from eight *tons* of pitchblende.

Three years later came an electrifying breakthrough, when Albert Einstein published his theory of relativity. The twenty-six-year-old German Jew, who would be forced into exile by Adolf Hitler in 1933, asserted that matter (mass) and energy were two forms of the same thing. According to Einstein, if somehow we could transform mass into energy, it would be possible to "liberate" amounts of energy incalculably greater than that generated by traditional methods—as by burning coal, for instance. Einstein's famous formula, $E=mc^2$ (energy equals mass multiplied by the square of the speed of light) gave some idea of how large this gain would be. This means that a single gram of matter has locked within it, in a frozen state, 25 million kilowatt-hours of energy—about what Grand Coulee Dam produces from sunup to sundown. Within a decade people were speculating that someday ships might cross the ocean fueled by the atomic energy contained in something no bigger than a lump of coal.

It was one thing to know that something *could* be done; quite another, however, to do it. How did one convert "mass" into "energy"? To begin with, scientists had to know exactly what it was they were converting. During the second decade of the century, a major step was taken in that direction when Ernest Rutherford and Niels Bohr described the structure of an atom more precisely. It was made up, they said, of a *positively charged core*—or *nucleus*—which constituted almost all of its "mass," and of *negatively charged electrons* that revolved around the nucleus. It was this nucleus, scientists concluded, that had to be broken, disintegrated, "exploded," if atomic energy was to be liberated.

In the 1930's physicists finally zeroed in on their goal. In 1932, James Chadwick discovered the *neutron*—a particle without electric charges, which was present in the nucleus along with positively charged *protons*. Two years later Enrico Fermi in Italy and Irène and Frédéric Joliot-Curie in France both disintegrated heavy atoms by spraying them with neutrons. Unfortunately they didn't realize they had achieved nuclear fission. In December 1938, however, Otto Hahn and Fritz Strassman in Berlin did a similar experiment with uranium and were able to verify a world-shaking achievement. They had split an atom. *They had produced nuclear fission.* They had transformed mass into energy—thirty-three years after Einstein said it *could* be done.

Nuclear fission was an exciting discovery—so much so that within a year a hundred articles were published on the subject in scientific journals. But to put fission to practical use—say, to generate electricity or to produce an atomic bomb—still presented knotty problems. One was to determine whether a *chain reaction* could be induced. In the process of "exploding" a single uranium atom, would some of the neutrons in its nucleus be freed to disintegrate nearby atoms?

In March 1939, Leo Szilard, a Hungarian-born physicist who had once worked with Einstein in Berlin, and Fermi conducted experiments at Columbia University in New York. They proved what they had suspected—that in the process of nuclear fission, neutrons were emitted. A chain reaction indeed was possible. Szilard watched as flashes of light on the screen confirmed his experiments were a success. He was now convinced "that atomic energy was possible in our lifetime." But he also had a premonition of tragedy. "That night," Szilard later recalled, "I knew the world was headed for sorrow."

It was already headed for sorrow in another sense. In slightly more than five months German troops would be marching into Poland and World War II would begin, ultimately taking 52 million lives. Science was made to serve politics. If an atomic bomb could, in fact, be built, the side that had it first would have an enormous advantage—perhaps enough to force the other side to surrender. Szilard and two other émigrés from Hungary, Edward Teller and Eugene Wigner, feared that the odds were with Nazi Germany. Its scientists had achieved nuclear fission first; moreover, it controlled uranium mines in Czechoslovakia and might seize those of the Belgian Congo (now Zaire), the world's largest source of this relatively scarce element. That seemed to give Germany a big head start.

Szilard and Wigner conveyed their concern to Einstein, who was then teaching at Princeton University, and asked him to communicate with President Franklin D. Roosevelt. On August 2, 1939—a landmark of sorts—the noted physicist wrote a letter to the American President. "In the course of the last four months," he said, "it has been made probable—through the work of Joliot in France as well as Fermi and Szilard in America —that it may become possible to set up nuclear chain reactions in a large mass of uranium. . . . This new phenomenon would also lead to the construction of bombs. . . . A single bomb of this type, carried by boat or exploded in a port, might very well destroy the whole port together with some of the surrounding territory." Einstein noted that Germany had stopped the sale of uranium, a strong hint that it might be planning to use that element for atomic bombs. He urged Roosevelt to begin a nuclear program without delay.

It is ironic that Einstein wrote this letter. The famed physicist was a pacifist—opposed to war as a matter of principle. He was the last person in the world one would expect to promote the most frightening weapon in all history. Moreover, as it turned out, his fears—and those of Szilard—were unfounded. Germany made no plans to produce a nuclear weapon during the war; its leaders were convinced it could not be done in so short a time.

In later years Einstein deplored the role he had played: "I made one great mistake in my life," he told Linus Pauling, another prominent scientist, "when I signed the letter to President Roosevelt recommending that atom bombs be made." But in the feverish days of 1939 many people were afraid that Hitlerism might sweep the planet, snuffing out democratic freedoms wherever it prevailed. Einstein's letter reflected that anxiety.

Roosevelt gave the note to an aide with the notation: "This requires action." Thus began the nuclear age. For the next six years scientists, engineers, generals, government officials joined hands in the Manhattan Project—a massive enterprise to produce an atomic bomb. Sometimes the pace was slow, especially at the beginning, when even Fermi had doubts that the job could be done. In its later stages the pace was feverish.

The government spent more than $2 billion constructing a number of special research laboratories, hiring scientists and engineers, and building thirty-seven installations in nineteen states and Canada. Oddly enough, despite the scope of the effort, the secret was so well kept that practically no one outside a small select circle knew what was going on.

The two major problems that remained to be solved were (1) how to draw from nature the scarce fuel needed to make a nuclear bomb, and (2) how to cause an explosion with that fuel.

The basic material—uranium—was not hard to find. Most of it was imported at first from the Belgian Congo. But uranium in its natural form—uranium-238—cannot be used for either bombs or energy. It is only slightly radioactive. In every hundred pounds of natural uranium, however, there is seven tenths of a pound of a fissionable and radioactive isotope, uranium-235. To be usable in power reactors (that make electricity), uranium must be enriched by a complicated chemical process, so that the proportion of U-235 grows to 3 or 4 percent of the uranium in the fuel rods. For the bomb it must be enriched still further, to as much as 90 percent, leaving only 10 percent U-238.

As early as April 1940, British scientists—most of them also refugees from Hitler—found a means by which U-235 could be separated from U-238. In time the United States built three "enrichment" plants for that purpose—at Oak Ridge, Tennessee; Portsmouth, Ohio; and Paducah, Kentucky.

A second major problem was how to explode the U-235. The neutrons had to be used in such a way that they would fission a large number of atoms; they could not be allowed to escape without inducing a chain reaction. A first step toward solving this difficulty was achieved by Fermi and his international group of scientists on December 2, 1942. Under the stands of Stagg Field (a football stadium) of the University of Chicago, they secretly built an "atomic pile." Stacking graphite 19 feet high and 24½ feet on each side, they placed rods of uranium inside, interspersed with cadmium rods to control the experiment.

Watching from a balcony, Fermi's team could see on their instruments a buildup of neutrons and, when the cadmium rods were removed, a controlled chain reaction—the first one in history. One of the by-products of the experiment was a highly radioactive element not found in nature—plutonium-239. Pu-239—which is intensely radioactive for tens of thousands of years—is, like U-235, another substance out of which nuclear bombs are made.

Having passed this milestone—a controlled chain reaction—the Manhattan Project scientists set to work on the final part of the puzzle: how to explode the nuclear fuel. A pound of U-235 is the size of a golf ball, but unlike a pound of TNT, it cannot be made to blow up. It won't sustain a chain reaction because too many neutrons escape this small mass. The physicists found they needed about ten pounds of U-235 (the size of a baseball) to achieve *critical mass*. "The trick in making a bomb," writes Dr. Ralph Lapp, one of the scientists on the Manhattan Project, "is to create a mechanism which will trigger an explosion by bringing the critical mass together suddenly." While big production plants at Oak Ridge, Tennessee, and Hanford, Washington, provided the fissionable U-235 and Pu-239, mathematicians, engineers, physicists, chemists, and other scientists, experimented with bomb designs at the Los Alamos Laboratory near Sante Fe, New Mexico. By July 1945 they had produced a device they called the "Fat Man" and were ready for the first nuclear explosion.

Waiting for the test to take place on July 16, 1945—at an airbase in Alamogordo, New Mexico—the scientists were both elated and troubled. As they stood in the desert that morning they wondered about how big an area the bomb would destroy. An atomic weapon, it will be recalled, gains its awesome power from a chain reaction. As neutrons shatter the nucleus of a uranium or plutonium atom, more neutrons are freed to disintegrate other nuclei—and so on. But how far would this chain reaction go? Would it stop at some point, or go on indefinitely?

Dr. Arthur H. Compton, director of the atomic energy program at the University of Chicago, had already discussed this matter with J. Robert Oppenheimer, scientific chief of the project. The two men speculated on how a chain reaction might affect the hydrogen in seawater. Might not the explosion of the atomic bomb, they asked themselves, set off an explosion of the ocean itself? Oppenheimer was worried because nitrogen in the air is also unstable. "Might not it, too," he speculated, "be set off by an atomic explosion in the atmosphere?" Conceivably the planet itself could be "vaporized." Such a result obviously would be the ultimate catastrophe, the two men agreed.

Author Stephane Groueff records in her book *Manhattan Project: The Untold Story of the Making of the Atomic Bomb* that on the morning of the big test Fermi was "making bets with his colleagues on whether the bomb would ignite the atmosphere, and, if so, whether it would destroy only New Mexico—or the entire world." Tortured by such questions, Compton ordered a recalculation of the possibility of such an accident. If it were proved that the chances were more than approximately three in one million, he said, he would scrap the test.

One can only speculate as to the reaction of the American people if they had known about Compton's dilemma that July morning. Perhaps a majority would have argued that the chances of the world's blowing up were too small to worry about, and that the test should go on. But there undoubtedly would have been many—particularly since Germany had already surrendered—who would have said the risk was too great, and would have insisted that the test be canceled.

But the American people were not asked for their opinion; they did not know what was happening at Alamogordo. Compton's recomputation was done quickly. It showed that there were fewer than three chances in a million that the entire world would blow up. So the first nuclear device in history—"Fat Man"—was set off. Oppenheimer, watching the huge ball of fire mushrooming across the New Mexico desert, recalled a line of Oriental poetry: "Now I am become death, destroyer of worlds." In a message to President Harry Truman, General Leslie R. Groves reported that "the test was successful beyond the most optimistic expectations of anyone." The blast, he said, was equal to that of 15,000 to 20,000 tons of TNT.

The most powerful bomb ever used in warfare previously had been the "blockbuster" of World War II; it contained ten tons of TNT. The new weapon was 1,500 to 2,000 times more powerful, and within a decade there would be nuclear weapons a million, two million, even five million times more powerful. The implications for warfare, diplomacy, human health, law, and democracy would be truly revolutionary. As Secretary Stimson had said a few weeks before, the bomb represented a change in the relations between man and the universe.

As it became evident that the United States would produce a nuclear bomb before the end of the war, a number of scientists, military men, and political leaders expressed second thoughts about using the weapon. For one thing, there no longer was a sense of urgency. Germany and Italy had already surrendered; Japan, with most of its navy and air force already destroyed, was certain to do the same very soon.

A half dozen groups of scientists recommended that the bomb not be dropped on Japan. The most militant of these was headed by a Nobel laureate, Dr. James Franck of the University of Chicago. His committee warned the President that science could not guarantee a defense against atom bombs—as it had against airplanes, tanks, submarines, and other weapons. Unless the atom bomb was placed under international control, said the Franck group, there would be an intense "race for nuclear armaments"—leading ultimately to a new and more devastating war. Instead of targeting the bomb against Japanese cities, they urged the United States to explode it "on the desert or a barren island" to demonstrate its frightening power. Japan would get the message—and give up.

Szilard and two of his associates made the same points in a meeting with James F. Byrnes, the designated Secretary of State. But to no avail. Subsequently they circulated a petition urging President Truman to rule out the use of atomic bombs because it would open the "door to an era of devastation of an unimaginable scale."

Like the many scientists who signed petitions, military leaders were also lukewarm about the bomb—originally. General Dwight D. Eisenhower, former commander of the allied armies in Europe, records that he had "a feeling of depression" when he was told by Secretary Stimson that the bomb was about to be dropped on Japan. "I voiced to him my grave misgivings," Eisenhower writes, because "Japan was already defeated . . . it wasn't necessary to hit them with that awful thing." It would only shock world opinion, the future President argued. Fleet Admiral William F. Halsey, Jr., later called the bombing of Hiroshima "an unnecessary experiment. It was a mistake to . . . drop it." Similar sentiments were expressed by General Curtis E. LeMay, General Henry H. (Hap) Arnold, and Admirals William D. Leahy and Ernest J. King.

The Truman administration, however, had other ideas. It was not just a matter of using the bomb to defeat Japan. "The bomb might well put us in a position to dictate our own terms at the end of war," Byrnes told Truman, "because we wouldn't have to make concessions to Russia or anyone else. Our possessing and demonstrating the bomb," he said, "would make Russia more manageable in Europe."

Secretary Stimson shared this view. The United States, he told Truman, had two bargaining chips as far as Russia was concerned: a vastly stronger economy and the bomb. Tho- chips, he explained, were "a royal flush, and we mustn't be fool about the way we play it." Bernard Baruch, well-known financier and Presidential adviser, expressed the general mood in Truman's inner circle thusly: "America can get what she wants if she insists on it. After all, we've got it—the bomb—and they [the Russians] haven't and won't have it for a long time to come." Hard-line American officials believed that Russia was so far behind in nuclear science that it would be a generation before it could make a nuclear weapon. General Groves thought it would take the Soviet Union from twenty to fifty years. "Why, those people can't even make a Jeep," he said.

President Truman brushed aside all suggestions that the bomb not be used—or that it be exploded in a remote desert to demonstrate to the Japanese what would befall them if they didn't surrender. "Let there be no mistake about it," he reminisced years later. "I regarded the bomb as a military weapon and never had any doubt that it should be used." A week after the test at Alamogordo, Secretary Stimson was advised that one uranium bomb would be ready on August 1, a plutonium bomb a few days later, and a third atomic weapon on August 24. Four targets had already been chosen; they fulfilled the criterion Stimson had set in May: a military center surrounded by working-class homes.

On August 6, 1945, two B-29 aircraft, taking off from an American-occupied island in the Pacific, headed for Hiroshima. One of them, christened *Enola Gay* by its captain, Paul W. Tibbets, Jr., carried the first nuclear weapon to be used against a living city. At 8:50 A.M. the planes passed over Japan's main island, unchallenged—the Japanese air force was virtually wiped out. At 9:11 A.M. the *Enola Gay* made a four-minute trial run over Hiroshima, maneuvered the cross hairs on its bombsight, and released a 13-kiloton nuclear bomb (equal in firepower to 13,000 tons of TNT).

For ten or fifteen seconds, as the small sphere fell toward the ground, people below didn't suspect that something horrible was about to happen. The crew inside the *Enola Gay* could see a pinpoint of purplish red. Then suddenly it expanded into a ball of fire a half mile in diameter, climbing until it was ten miles above ground—and still growing. Anyone who looked directly into the ball was instantly blinded. It was brighter, someone later wrote, than a thousand suns.

The blast and fire consumed people as if they had been pulverized or cremated. Thousands left no remains, except perhaps black shadows on the stones. Everywhere people were running frenziedly toward the seven rivers in and around the city, but even those who could cool themselves for the moment died a month later from the irradiated and poisoned water. Walls of flame, higher than big buildings, trapped thousands. For miles around, buildings, cars, trucks, homes were flattened, and human beings and their possessions were tossed hundreds of feet into the air like projectiles. An area of four square miles in the center of town was totally demolished; 90 percent of the remainder was in ruins.

A survivor later described the scene to Dr. Robert Jay Lifton: "The appearance of people was . . . well, they all had skin blackened by burns. . . . They had no hair because their hair was burned, and at a glance you couldn't tell whether you were looking at them from in front or in back. . . . They held their arms bent . . . and their skin—not only on their hands, but on their faces and bodies too—hung down. . . . Wherever I walked I met these people. . . . Many of them died along the road— I can still picture them in my mind—like walking ghosts. . . . They didn't look like people of this world. . . . They had a special way of walking—very slowly. . . . I myself was one of them."

The Interim Committee in Washington had expected that 20,000 people would die. In fact, 142,000 perished, including two American Navy fliers who were in the city jail; 62,000 buildings and homes were pulverized.

Returning home aboard the cruiser *Augusta,* after a seventeen-day meeting with Winston Churchill and Joseph Stalin in Potsdam, Germany, President Truman was handed a note. The *Enola Gay,* it said, had accomplished its mission. Turning to a group of sailors, the President exclaimed, "This is the greatest thing in history."

On August 9 the same scenario was reenacted over Nagasaki. The target in this raid was to have been Kokura, but clouds obscured the city as two B-29's approached it. Since orders had been given to make only a visual drop, the pilot of the lead plane headed toward the secondary target, Nagasaki. At 12:01 P.M. that day a black object fell out of the belly of "No. 77," and in a few seconds there was a tremendous flash, followed by great blast waves that made even the attacking airplanes tremble. A ball of purple fire, visible from the tail of the airplanes, rose tens of thousands of feet into the air. The great mushroom cloud, according to a newspaper correspondent who flew with the second plane, "assumed the form of a giant square totem pole, with its base about three miles long, tapering off to about a mile at the top. Its bottom was brown, its center amber, its top white."

Below, as at Hiroshima, was utter chaos: blackened bodies, men and women on fire, people searching aimlessly for loved ones or slowly succumbing to radiation. The death toll at Nagasaki was about half that of Hiroshima—75,000—perhaps because the drop was a mile off target. Had it been three miles off target in the other direction, it might have killed a thousand Americans who were being held there as prisoners of war.

On August 14, Japan surrendered.

Historians and political scientists are still arguing as to whether it was necessary to use atomic bombs on Hiroshima and Nagasaki. Everyone agrees that Japan would have given up fairly soon. In fact, it had already made overtures for surrender through Swedish and Soviet intermediaries. But President Truman and Secretary Stimson claimed that the United States would have had to invade Japan with combat troops, and in the process would have suffered a million casualties. Karl T. Compton, president of the Massachusetts Institute of Technology, put the estimate at "hundreds of thousands—perhaps several million." In 1949, President Truman cut his estimate to 200,000.

On the other hand, a Strategic Bombing Survey group of experts sent to Japan in 1946 came to a different conclusion. It stated that "the Hiroshima and Nagasaki atomic bombs did not defeat Japan, nor, by the testimony of the enemy leaders who ended the war, did they persuade Japan to accept unconditional surrender." In the survey's opinion, Japan would have surrendered "in all probability prior to 1 November 1945 . . . even if the atomic bombs had not been dropped, even if Russia had not entered the war, and even if no invasion had been planned or contemplated."

3. THE BOMB THAT DIDN'T

"ONE NATION CANNOT DEFEAT ANOTHER NATION TODAY. THAT CONCEPT DIED WITH HIROSHIMA." General Henry H. (Hap) Arnold

Since August 9, 1945, no nuclear bombs have been used on people anywhere. But the bomb continued to stir up controversy. In mid-1945 the dispute had been about dropping the weapon on human beings. After the war it centered on whether to disarm or to expand the nuclear program. The decision by President Truman to make the bomb the centerpiece of United States foreign and military policy changed the American way of life in ways that few people could anticipate.

The first postwar disagreement concerning the bomb came early. Surprisingly, it was initiated by the man who just recently had given the final orders for dropping atom bombs on Hiroshima and Nagasaki. On September 11, 1945, less than a month after hostilities ended, Secretary of War Stimson wrote a memorandum to President Truman. The secretary, a former Wall Street lawyer, then seventy-seven years old, was about to leave office after decades of service in the government. "The advent of the atomic bomb," he wrote Truman, ". . . has profoundly affected political considerations in all sections of the globe." True, the United States enjoyed "momentary superiority" because it had the bomb, but the Soviets were bound to learn "the necessary secrets of production" in four to twenty years. The choice for the United States, then, was either to form an atomic partnership with Moscow now and secure its cooperation for an enduring worldwide peace, or to provoke "a secret armament race of a rather desperate character." The secretary proposed an atomic partnership.

Stimson urged Truman to stop producing nuclear weapons, to impound those already stockpiled, and to confine his nuclear program to "commercial or humanitarian purposes," such as generating electricity.

Stimson also made some interesting comments about trust. Could Washington trust the Russians? He knew that Truman was hostile to the Soviet leadership. Eleven days after becoming Chief Executive in April 1945, Truman had told an American diplomat, Charles E. Bohlen, that "if the Russians did not wish to join us they could go to hell." That same day he had dressed down the Soviet foreign minister, Vyacheslav Molotov, in what Bohlen called "Missouri mule driver's language." And two weeks later he had terminated all lend-lease aid to the Russians.

But Stimson felt this was the wrong approach. It was urgent to come to an understanding with the Russians, and to do that, you had to trust them. "The chief lesson I have learned in a long life," he said in his letter to Truman, "is that the only way you can make a man trustworthy is to trust him; and the surest way to make him untrustworthy is to distrust him and show your distrust." Stimson's proposal for atomic partnership received support within the Truman Cabinet from Secretary of Commerce Henry Wallace, Secretary of Labor Lewis Schwellenbach, and Postmaster General Robert Hannegan. But, as the saying goes, it did not fly; Truman rejected it.

An even more drastic plan leading to nuclear disarmament was the call for world government. Among the many intellectuals who supported this idea was—as might be expected—Albert Einstein. "As long as there are sovereign nations possessing great power," Einstein wrote in November 1945, "war is inevitable." And, in the atomic age, that "would lead to the destruction of a large part of the world's population, cities, and industrial resources." In Einstein's view there was "no conceivable cause which could justify so great a sacrifice."

The only way to prevent it, said the German-born physicist, was to form a world government that would have a monopoly on military power. In other words, there would no longer be any nations in the sense we know them today—each with its own army, navy, and air force. All would give up their armed forces to the international government, and thus would never again be able to make war against one another. Einstein admitted there was a danger that world government might become a tyranny. But even that was preferable to another war, with the "intensified destructiveness" of nuclear weapons.

Supporting the cause of world government was a prestigious group of scientists and intellectuals. In 1946 they published a paperback book called *One World or None.* As the title suggests, they argued that unless the nations of the world formed a single world government, atomic war would someday destroy the planet. Hence the choice in a real sense was between one world and none. Among the contributors to this book were Niels Bohr, J. Robert Oppenheimer, Leo Szilard, the famed columnist Walter Lippmann, and the Federation of American Scientists.

Taking a pro-nuclear position was Harry Truman. It wasn't that the President was insensitive to the horrors of atomic war. In his memoirs he records that "ever since Hiroshima I had never stopped thinking about the frightful implications of the atomic bomb. We knew that this revolutionary scientific creation could destroy civilization." But Truman had no faith in a partnership with the Soviet Union. He distrusted its leaders; he was incensed about Soviet behavior in Poland and other Eastern European states. In a letter to Secretary of State Byrnes, he argued that "unless Russia is faced with an iron fist and strong language, war is in the making . . . I'm tired of babying the Soviets."

Fortifying Truman's position was the belief that the United States could not be challenged by any nation—including the Soviet Union—for decades to come. Prevailing opinion in the administration was that the Russians wouldn't be able to make an atom bomb for a generation or more. Meanwhile America would enjoy a monopoly of the most fearsome weapon in history—and would be able to organize the postwar world around American principles of "free trade" and "free enterprise."

The Soviet Union, it was believed, could not stop the United States. Apart from the fact that it did not have the bomb as yet, it had been greatly weakened by World War II. Twenty million Russians had been killed. Fifteen large cities, 1,710 towns, and 70,000 villages had been partly or wholly destroyed. Six million buildings had been demolished, 10,000 power stations ruined.

Under these circumstances, the bomb gave Truman a sense of power. In the first test of that power Moscow backed off—reinforcing Truman's faith in the bomb. Early in 1946 the United States and the Soviet Union had a dispute over Soviet troops in Iran. The dispute went back to 1941, when Iran's ruler, Riza Shah Pahlavi, indicated he would side with Hitler in World War II. Since this would close off an important supply route into the Soviet Union and might endanger British oil holdings in Iran, both British and Soviet forces decided to occupy Iran.

The Russians took over the northern part of the country, whereas the British occupied the central and southern sections (in which their oil fields lay). By the terms of a wartime treaty all three nations (including the United States which also occupied part of the country) were obligated to withdraw their forces no later than six months after the war. But when the time came—March 2, 1946—the British and Americans evacuated Iran, but the Soviets balked. In the meantime they had encouraged a revolt in the northern province of Azerbaijan, had installed a pro-Communist government under Jafar Pishevari, and had secured a temporary concession to explore for oil. This was important for Moscow because it had suffered heavy losses in its own oil fields.

Legally, of course, the Soviets were in the wrong. But British and other Allied troops were still ensconced in Greece, Syria, Lebanon, Indochina, the Dutch East Indies, and elsewhere. The Soviets considered it unfair that they were being pressured to give up their prize, especially since, before 1918, Iran had been a Russian sphere of influence.

Truman, however, would accept no excuses. Summoning Soviet Ambassador Andrei Gromyko to the White House, the President delivered an ultimatum. If the Russians did not evacuate Azerbaijan, the United States would attack the Soviet Union itself with atom bombs. "We're going to drop it on you," the President told Gromyko. The Russians yielded; they withdrew their troops shortly thereafter.

America's monopoly of the bomb buoyed the mood that "we're not afraid of anyone." Expressing that mood in the intimate circles of the Truman administration was a 1946 secret report by a young White House counsel named Clark Clifford. Titled "A Summary of American Relations with the Soviet Union," Clifford's paper was based on interviews with the Secretaries of State, War, and Navy, the Attorney General, the Joint Chiefs of Staff, Fleet Admiral William D. Leahy, and the director of Central Intelligence, among others. All expressed "a remarkable agreement," Clifford wrote, that "the U.S., with a military potential composed primarily of highly effective weapons, should entertain no proposal for disarmament or limitation of armament." It should refuse to outlaw "atomic warfare and long-range offensive weapons." He concluded that "the U.S. must be prepared to wage atomic and biological warfare."

There were other sharp voices in the American leadership. Two months after Japan surrendered, General George S. Patton urged the United States government to remain armed and prepared for an "inevitable" new war. General Henry H. (Hap) Arnold of the Air Force proposed offensive readiness. "We must use our most brilliant scientists," he said, "to develop better weapons more quickly and more effectively. We must take advantage of the bases we now have to be closer to an enemy's vital points with our weapons than he is to ours. We must use the most modern weapons of all kinds, so that we can beat any potential opponent to the draw." Since the Soviet Union was the only "potential opponent," it was obvious he was talking of a possible war with the Kremlin.

Later, the nation began to hear a new term—"preventative war." Major General Orville A. Anderson, commandant of the Air War College, was generally considered the strongest advocate of preventative war. He often lectured on the advisability of launching an A-bomb attack on Russia. "Which is the greater immorality," he asked, "preventative war as a means to keep the U.S.S.R. from becoming a nuclear power, or to allow a totalitarian dictatorial system to develop a means whereby the free world could be intimidated, blackmailed, and possibly destroyed?" The question answered itself. Anderson considered a surprise attack—a preventative war—against Russia the lesser of two evils. The Truman administration felt he had gone too far and suspended him in September 1950 for airing such views. But other, and even more influential, voices suggested the same policy.

On August 25, 1950, Secretary of the Navy Francis Matthews told an audience of 100,000 in Omaha that he advocated "a war to compel co-operation for peace. . . . We would become the *first aggressors for peace"* [emphasis added]. Defense Secretary Louis A. Johnson concurred in these views. As outlined to a newspaper columnist, the United States would give the Soviet Union an ultimatum to disarm. If the Soviets refused, as expected, Washington would declare war and unleash its atom bombs to destroy Russian military power.

President Truman never took the path suggested by these extreme elements. The administration was ready to wage "atomic and biological" war, if necessary. But cool reflection indicated that the results of such a course would be questionable. At the time the United States was producing only enough nuclear material—uranium 235 and plutonium—to make one hundred A-bombs a year. That would surely hurt the Soviet Union, but it was not enough to destroy it—especially since some of the American bombers would be shot down before they reached their targets. The intercontinental ballistic missile had not yet been invented, and much slower American bombers would have to contend with excellent Soviet fighter planes.

The best we could hope for would be to "wound" the Soviet Union; we didn't have sufficient weaponry, atomic or otherwise, to force it to surrender. Meanwhile—and this is the important point—the Red Army would be able to overrun all of Western Europe to the English Channel. As one of Europe's most authoritative writers, Raymond Aron, put it: "United States superiority over the Soviet Union in the nuclear field was offset . . . by Russian superiority in conventional arms and by the Red Army's continued ability to overrun Western Europe in a matter of days. . . ."

A secret report of the National Security Council in April 1950—NSC-68—made the same point. "The Soviet Union and its satellites," it said, had the capability "to overrun Western Europe, with the possible exception of the Iberian and Scandinavian Peninsulas." United States victory was out of the question. "A powerful blow could be delivered upon the Soviet Union," said the report, "but it is estimated that these operations alone would not force or induce the Kremlin to capitulate." The final decision, then, would rest on whether the United States Army could hold back Soviet conventional forces. That was not very likely. As General George C. Kenney, Commander of the Strategic Air Force, noted: "The United States has no intention of landing mass armies in Europe and slugging it out with the Red Army—manpower against manpower. Napoleon and Hitler both made that mistake."

The bomb obviously had limitations. It did not always ensure success.

The Truman administration recognized this fact. It was prepared to use nuclear weapons if necessary, but it settled for a broader policy, called "containment." As explained by its prime theorist, George F. Kennan, containment included the idea that the United States would withhold strategic goods and know-how from the Soviet Union. And it would place other pressures on Moscow, including military pressures, so as to "increase enormously the strains under which the Soviet policy must operate." This would create problems within the Soviet sphere that would eventually cause either "the breakup or the gradual mellowing of Soviet power."

Meanwhile Truman continued to build the atomic arsenal, and continued research for even more potent nuclear weapons.

Given this emphasis on the bomb as the cornerstone of American security, it was only natural that Washington would take steps to prevent the Soviet Union from learning the secret of how to produce one. Everyone, of course, knew the general scientific principles behind the weapon—such as the principle of relativity. But there were more specific scientific and engineering problems to be considered. How much uranium-235 or plutonium was needed for a single bomb? What configuration of such fuels could bring about "critical mass"? And so on. The United States had that knowledge: the Soviet Union did not.

Safeguarding the secret, then, became an obsessive concern for the United States government—and it brought about drastic changes in the way the government operated. In a message to Congress less than two months after the war ended, Truman warned that atomic secrets must be kept from "ignorant or evil hands" lest they "inflict untold disaster upon the nation and the world."

An Atomic Energy Act passed some months later contained provisions unique to the American way of life. To begin with, it established an Atomic Energy Commission with full control over research, development, and production of nuclear bombs. After previous wars the government usually reduced ordnance operations; this time it created a permanent institution for producing atomic weaponry. Equally important, the AEC was empowered to keep its research secret, a policy that scientists have always opposed. As of 1949 the AEC had 308,000 reports in its files; 90 percent of them marked "secret."

Most important of all, the act prescribed punishment more severe than existed even under the Espionage Act. Under the latter the death penalty could be imposed only in time of war, but under the Atomic Energy Act a person could be hanged for revealing atomic secrets in peacetime. America had never had so severe a law. Indeed the act was so sweeping, it punished people even for being careless or indiscrete. To indicate how far afield this obsession with secrecy went, on one occasion AEC ordered General Electric to refuse collective bargaining rights at Defense Plants to the United Electrical Workers Union (UE). Even though the union was chosen by GE's workers in an election, AEC charged that UE's leaders were radicals and might betray secrets.

To guard the mounting heap of secrets, the government also instituted "loyalty" and "security" programs. Three months after the Atomic Energy Act became law, Truman issued Executive Order No. 9835, which called for investigation of federal employees and those applying for federal jobs to see if they were "loyal." Before 1939 a federal employee merely took an oath to defend the Constitution. A long-standing civil service rule prohibited the government from asking about "political or religious opinions or affiliations."

Executive Order 9835 demolished that principle. The Attorney General prepared a list of two hundred organizations that he described as "totalitarian, fascist, communist, or subversive." Anyone associated with such organizations would lose his or her government job. He or she could appeal the ruling, but the government did not have to produce the informer so that the employee could confront his accuser. Thus, without trial, a person could be denied a job with the government simply for *believing* in a set of ideas, not necessarily *doing* anything illegal. In the first five years after Truman's order, the FBI investigated 4 million applicants and employees. (The question about loyalty on federal job application forms survived until mid-1976, when the American Civil Liberties Union won two court decisions to remove it.)

"Loyalty" became something of a mania, applied in a loose

and haphazard manner. James Kutcher, a war veteran who had lost both his legs in the 1943 battle of San Pietro in Italy, was fired from a clerk's job in the Newark office of the Veterans Administration. He was a member of the Socialist Workers party, a small group that followed the teachings of Leon Trotsky. Ironically, it is still a *legal* party today, and it regularly runs candidates for public office. Lieutenant Milo J. Radulovich, whose own loyalty was never questioned, was discharged from the Air Force because his father read a Slavic-language newspaper that was pro-Communist, and his sister allegedly associated with "Communist-fronts."

Before long the "loyalty" program spread from government to other sectors. Employers used the Attorney General's list of two hundred "subversive" organizations as a guide for hiring and firing. A million tenants in government-financed buildings were required to sign loyalty oaths that they were not Communists—or lose their apartments. Soon loyalty oaths were demanded of teachers in public schools and professors at universities, maritime workers, workers in defense factories and, in Indiana, even of prizefighters and wrestlers. Under the 1947 Taft-Hartley Act, union officials had to swear they were not members of subversive organizations or lose the right to represent their members before the National Labor Relations Board.

All of this, of course, was far afield from safeguarding the secret of the bomb—but it grew out of it. Beginning in 1950, the government took another step to ensure "loyalty." Under the prodding of Congressman Richard Nixon, a "security risk" program was introduced. Now the government fired people it feared might become "disloyal" in the future. The person discharged need not actually be a problem today, but if his superiors and the FBI felt there was a *risk* in keeping him, he could be fired. Thus many homosexuals were discharged on the theory they were vulnerable to blackmail by foreign powers or subversives. There was no appeal.

This, too, was unique in the American experience. So was the withholding of information from the public. The government, of course, had kept certain things secret since the beginning of the Republic—for instance, war plans. But the secrecy never took on the proportions it did during the nuclear age. The Atomic Energy Act cut off one big source of information from public review. So did the National Security Act of 1947, the Internal Security Act of 1950, and a number of executive orders.

Most significant was Executive Order 10501, issued by President Eisenhower, which gave leading government agencies the right to classify government papers as "secret," "top secret," "confidential," "classified," et cetera. Tens of millions of documents were thereby kept from the citizenry. Critics charged that the American people needed to know more about what their government was doing and thinking—if they were to influence national decisions and elect the right people. But the practice of secrecy not only continued, but broadened.

In many—probably most—instances the classified documents were not withheld because they might feed intelligence to the Russians, but because they were embarrassing to American officials. For instance, the menu for a dinner given Queen Frederika of Greece was stamped "classified" —evidently to prevent the press from commenting on how lavish it was. A "secret" label was attached to *newspaper* clippings about a Navy communications project in Wisconsin. The National Security Agency, the most secret of all United States intelligence agencies, was established by executive order—and not law—on November 4, 1952; its very existence was not acknowledged for five years.

The National Security Act of 1947 added to the secrecy mania when it established two agencies of government that by their very nature had to be secretive. The National Security Council is charged with coordinating "domestic, foreign, and military policies." The NSC could not publicly admit, for instance, that it had instructed the CIA to give arms to a group trying to overthrow the legal government of Chile or Brazil. So it functions in the shadows. The Central Intelligence Agency, which is subordinate to the NSC, is the operating arm for spying and covert action; its functions are kept secret because they are often illegal. But the bomb was the seed out of which this new style of hidden government grew.

In the four years when the United States enjoyed a monopoly of the bomb—from 1945 to 1949—relations with the Soviet Union deteriorated. At first Joseph Stalin, the Soviet leader, displayed moderation—in part because he still hoped for United States economic help to rebuild his war-torn country. Under Stalin's pressure, for instance, Communists in France and Italy evacuated factories they had taken over at the end of the war and permitted their wartime military groups to be disarmed. In both countries the Communist party joined capitalist governments.

Soviet troops withdrew from Iran, Manchuria, Hungary, and Czechoslovakia. Though free elections were prohibited in most Soviet-controlled countries, they were permitted at first in Hungary. Here the small landholders' party received 59 percent of the vote, as against 17 percent for the Communist party. Free speech, free press, free elections, and a coalition government were tolerated in Czechoslovakia until February 1948. In Yugoslavia, Stalin even pressured Tito to allow monarchists into the government, and in China he urged Mao Tse-tung's Communists to stop fighting the conservative government headed by a United States ally, Chiang Kai-shek.

But the immediate postwar period was one of great social

upheaval. Nationalist movements were seeking independence in Madagascar, Algeria, Tunisia, and many other countries. Guerrillas were fighting France in Vietnam and threatening Holland in the Dutch East Indies. The British empire was shaken to its roots as India won its freedom and the British had to withdraw forces from other colonies.

Civil wars were going on in a half dozen places—Greece, the Philippines, Indochina, Korea, China. Each of these crises increased tensions between the United States and the Soviet Union. The Truman administration accused the Kremlin of encouraging left-wing rebels, hostile to the United States. The Kremlin accused Truman of supporting reaction, of being insensitive to human needs. What was already a bad situation became worse. East and West, in effect, became two separate worlds—the Soviet Union and its allies on the one side, the United States and its allies on the other. They were unable to come to terms on virtually anything—including disarmament.

In January 1946 President Truman appointed a committee to prepare a proposal for controlling the atom. Throughout Europe, and to some extent in the United States, groups were forming around the cry "Ban the Bomb." Many people had lost fathers in World War I and brothers in World War II. They were anxious to prevent World War III, especially a nuclear World War III. Truman paid heed to this sentiment by formulating a plan that financier Bernard Baruch presented to the United Nations in June 1946.

The Baruch Plan called for an international atomic development authority—under the United Nations—that would own and manage everything associated with atomic energy around the world, from the uranium mine to the bomb. But the Soviets (and some American leaders) objected to certain features of the proposal. For one thing, the United States would be allowed to continue production of nuclear weapons while inspectors were to be imposed on the Soviet Union. It was only at the end of a long process that the United States would stop producing the bomb and destroy its stockpile. Meanwhile, Moscow would have to scuttle its research and development.

One of the features of the Baruch Plan that particularly annoyed Stalin was the provision for "condign punishment" by the United Nations of any nation that violated the decisions of the international atomic development authority. Since the United Nations was then dominated by the United States (typical votes in the General Assembly were 40 to 6), the Kremlin feared that the plan would make it possible for the United States to mobilize the United Nations for war against the Soviet Union. Dean Acheson, Deputy Secretary of State, agreed with the Soviet position on this score. Such words, he said, would be "interpreted in Moscow only as an attempt to turn the United Nations into an alliance [to threaten] war against the USSR" unless it scrapped its own nuclear program.

In any case, no agreement was reached between the superpowers on nuclear disarmament in 1947. The two sides weren't talking *to* each other, but *at* each other. Neither side expected an agreement. Just seventeen days after the Baruch Plan was presented to the United Nations, the United States made clear it didn't intend to give up its nuclear lead. On July 1, 1946, it conducted the first postwar nuclear test over the Pacific island of Bikini.

The breach between East and West widened. Early in 1947, Britain ended military and economic aid to Greece. The United States took up Britain's role, and sent weapons and military advisers to Greece to help fight the EAM (communist) guerrillas. The President proclaimed the famous Truman Doctrine, offering help to governments fighting Communists.

A year or two later the Western nations formed a military alliance, the North Atlantic Treaty Organization, aimed at defending them from the Soviet Union—and internal Communists. Under United States leadership the West placed an embargo on selling strategic goods to Communist countries. The East responded by organizing a military alliance of its own, the Warsaw Pact, and by forming an agency called Comecon, to handle economic relations among nations in the Soviet orbit. Soviet attitudes hardened in response to a hardened American position. Bulgaria, Czechoslovakia, Hungary, and East Germany were proclaimed "people's republics"; dissent was further stifled, and many "soft" Communist leaders were either imprisoned or executed. In mid-1948, after a dispute between the Soviet Union and the United States over currency reform in occupied Germany, Soviet troops denied the West access into Berlin.

As in physics, each action had a reaction.

What is interesting is that the atom bomb played virtually no role in these events. It didn't strengthen the American hand. It didn't weaken the Soviet hand. Nor was it a factor, one way or the other, in two major setbacks suffered by the West in 1948–49.

In February 1948, Czechoslovak Communists rebelled against the regime of Eduard Benes, a non-Communist, and asserted full control over their country. In January 1949, Mao Tse-tung's Communists seized Peking, the capital of China, after a long civil war that had lasted a quarter of a century, and became the unchallenged rulers of the most populous nation on earth.

Then in August 1949, there was a third setback. Sometime between August 26 and 29, the Soviet Union detonated its first nuclear device. Instead of fifteen, twenty, or fifty years—as some American leaders had expected—the U.S.S.R. had caught up with the United States in just four years.

4. ANOTHER CHIP IN THE POT

"MODERN WEAPONS CONSTITUTE A TYPE OF BARBARISM
NOT WORTHY OF CIVILIZED MAN."   Admiral William Leahy

The Soviet Union kept its nuclear test secret—just as the United States had done four years earlier. But on September 3, 1949, American planes flying over Long Island collected an air sample that was highly radioactive. The Air Force then tracked a cloud of radioactive dust from the North Pacific to Great Britain. When scientists examined the samples there was no room for doubt: an atomic explosion had been set off in the Asiatic sector of the Soviet Union.

(Many years later, in 1972, a report for the House Committee on Foreign Affairs concluded that "Soviet development of atomic energy had proceeded quite well" until Russia became preoccupied with the war against Germany. "Soviet capability at that point [1941] has been estimated to have been on a par with that of the United States.")

The problem in 1949 was how to respond. What could—or should—the United States do about it? With another nation now possessing the bomb, America's nuclear threat was bound to lose some of its sting. Of course there was still the option of "atomic partnership" with the Soviet Union. But the mood of the nation was in the opposite direction. The conflict with the Soviet Union was being referred to as a "war"—the *Cold War.* And anti-communism was so severe that even Truman was castigated in some circles as "soft on communism." There was little hope, therefore, that the administration might reexamine its policy and conclude that the arms race was a mistake. The trend was toward "toughness."

As with the controversy over whether to use the A-bomb on Japan, the debate over how to respond to the Soviet breakthrough took place in the shadows. One group of scientists, including Edward Teller and Ernest O. Lawrence, urged the President to throw another military chip into the pot—what was then called the "Super." But this group was still a minority. Most of the nation's leading scientists feared the long-run consequences of the Super. They agreed that some kind of response to the Soviet test was necessary, but they didn't want to open a new chapter in the nuclear age.

The General Advisory Committee of the Atomic Energy Committee, made up of nine top scientists and chaired by J. Robert Oppenheimer, unanimously opposed the Super. Two of them, Enrico Fermi and I.I. Rabi, were particularly emphatic: "Necessarily such a weapon goes far beyond any military objective and enters the range of very great natural catastrophes. By its very nature it cannot be confined to a military objective but becomes a weapon which in practical effect is almost one of genocide." The Super, or hydrogen bomb, based on the principle of *fusion,* would ordinarily be a thousand times more powerful than the fission bomb. Such a weapon, argued Fermi and Rabi, "cannot be justified on any ethical ground. . . ."

Those who proposed to go ahead with the Super argued that it was only a matter of time before the Russians developed one.

Estimates were that it would take five years to produce the hydrogen bomb (actually it took less); if the Russians had one first, it would take too long for the United States to catch up. In the minds of men who considered themselves "practical," therefore, there was no alternative but to proceed. No public discussion took place, just as none had taken place on whether to produce and use the atomic bomb. On January 31, 1950, President Truman made the decision. "I believed," he writes in his memoirs, "that anything that would assure us the lead in the field of atomic energy development for defense had to be tried out. . . ."

The man usually referred to as the "father" of the Super—the hydrogen bomb—is Edward Teller. Like his friend Szilard, Teller was an emigré from Hungary. Up to a point his political evolution was also similar to Szilard's. He had urged the United States to initiate an atomic program in 1939, when it appeared that Hitler might acquire the fearful weapon first. When the bomb was near completion, however, he joined Szilard in a plea not to drop it on Japanese cities.

But his views changed shortly thereafter. He had become convinced that the bomb was "so terrible that no amount of protesting or fiddling with politics will save our souls." The only hope for human survival was to inform the public about the facts of atomic energy—and wait for its reaction. But that was not his—or Szilard's—function. A scientist's only job, he asserted, was to study "the laws of nature," not to make political decisions as to "whether a hydrogen bomb should be constructed or how it should be used."

Teller began thinking of a fusion bomb early in the 1940's. Scientists had known for decades that mass could be converted into vast amounts of energy. But it could be done in two different ways: One could take atoms of a heavy element such as uranium and break them up (fission), or take atoms of a light element such as hydrogen and fuse them (fusion). Fission, though complicated, was by far the easier process, but a fusion bomb could be a thousand times more powerful. In fact, as Hans Bethe noted in 1938, fusion was the means by which the sun itself produced heat and light.

Teller's ambitions were sidetracked for a period, while the scientific community concentrated on the fission bomb. But they were revived after the Soviet explosion of 1949. Even then, however, science still had to grapple with a number of thorny problems before the Super could be made.

One of them was what kind of fuel to use. Ordinary hydrogen, though light enough, could not be employed to make a hydrogen bomb any more than natural uranium (U-238) could be made into a fission bomb. Perhaps, suggested Enrico Fermi, deuterium—an isotope of hydrogen discovered by Harold Urey in 1932—could do the job. Deuterium, however, turned out to be insufficiently fusible. Next, attention fastened on another isotope, tritium, a form of hydrogen so rare in nature it had to be manufactured. But that would be costly and time-consuming. Finally, it was decided to use lithium deuteride, a solid compound made of lithium and deuterium. When the lithium 6 in this compound is split by neutrons, tritium is released. Thus the bomb makes its own fuel, its own energy.

Another problem was how to generate the multimillion-degree temperatures to fuse the light elements. There was nothing on earth that hot—except the atom bomb. The atom bomb, in fact, is the *trigger* for the hydrogen bomb. It provides the heat that fuses tritium and deuterium, and in the process releases innumerable fast neutrons both to explode the fuel and to fission the bomb's uranium jacket. The H-bomb, in fact, is not a fusion bomb per se, but a fission-fusion-fission bomb.

A third problem Teller and his associates grappled with is still considered so secret that the government has not yet released details about it—though many scientists know the "secret." In any case, Teller outlined a solution to it in the spring of 1951, and the project went into full swing.

On November 1, 1952, on a Pacific islet called Elugelab, in the Eniwetok atoll, American technicians detonated a 50-ton cubical box about two stories high, code-named Mike. Humankind had entered the second phase of the nuclear era, the hydrogen-bomb phase. As described by nuclear scientist Ralph Lapp, a massive fireball consumed the little island, "sucking up millions of tons of coral, and water turned to steam." A hundred thousand feet above ground the ball was three miles in diameter. Down below, nothing remained of the islet of Elugelab except a hole 175 feet deep and a mile in diameter. The adjacent island was "wiped clean"; had any human beings remained there, they would have instantly perished.

"Mike," the device that devastated Elugelab, had the power of 12 megatons (12 million tons of TNT); it was almost a thousand times more powerful than the A-bomb that had consumed Hiroshima seven years earlier. Sixteen months later the Pentagon tested an actual H-bomb, called "Bravo," on Bikini, an atoll in the Pacific. One of the lessons gleaned from this incident was that radioactive fallout extended over an area far larger than that caused by the blast.

The deadly dust from the explosion, says Herbert Scoville, one of the experts who checked Bravo's radioactivity, "was a big surprise to us." It covered an area of 7,000 square miles (30 times the size of Chicago), whereas the blast damaged 300 square miles. At the last minute the wind shifted to the east, where ten United States Task Force ships were within 30 miles. The crews hastened below as the ships sped away; and special equipment washed the decks with tons of water. A Japanese tuna boat, 90 miles from ground zero, did not fare so well; its 23 fishermen fell ill from the radiation—one is said to have died. Had the ship been ten miles south, all would have perished. A hundred miles from the explosion, a deserted island received eight times the lethal dose of radiation.

The nuclear race was now accelerating dramatically. Prior to 1949, the United States had tested one nuclear weapon in 1946, two in 1947, and three in 1948. In 1951, sixteen tests were conducted; in the following seven years, 150—66 in 1958 alone.

By now relations between the two superpowers were poisoned not only by the Soviet atomic test but by the war that began in Korea in June 1950. Seventy thousand Communist troops from North Korea crossed into South Korea. The United States, operating in the name of the United Nations, came to the aid of its ally in the South, and for the next three years fought an indecisive but costly war that took 54,246 American lives and many times that number of Korean lives. There remains some dispute as to how the war actually started, but support at home for the American cause was strong. So was hostility to the Soviet Union, with which North Korea was allied.

General Douglas MacArthur, in a May 1952 speech, described the national mood as "an artificially induced psychosis of war hysteria." "Our country is now geared," he said, "to an arms economy." United States military spending skyrocketed from $13 billion a year to $47 billion. A general estimate by 1960 was that the United States possessed thousands of nuclear warheads, perhaps as many as five thousand.

Whatever advantage the United States had gained from developing the hydrogen bomb was lost within nine months. In August 1953 the Russians, too, exploded a thermonuclear device. And within seven or eight years they accumulated a respectable stockpile of both hydrogen and atomic bombs. It was not nearly as large as the American arsenal, but it was formidable nonetheless.

Russian weapons tended to have more explosive power: in late 1961, for instance, the Soviet military exploded a 58-megaton bomb over the proving grounds at Novaya Zemlya, an archipelago in the Arctic Ocean. As of 1982, that was the most destructive thermonuclear weapon ever produced—equal to 58 million tons of TNT. Detonated high in the air, such a bomb could cause fires and fire storms sufficient to demolish a good-sized American state. American bombs, however, were more sophisticated and more accurate.

Both sides were now reaching the stage where each could inflict so much punishment on the other that a victory would be hollow. Military experts were beginning to talk of 20, 50, even 100 million deaths on each side in case of nuclear war.

Surveying the situation years later, Hans Bethe said: "The response the Government made in 1949 and 1950 to go ahead and develop the [hydrogen] bomb was natural and perhaps even correct. It was said then that we were in a Cold War and we had to develop the hydrogen bomb because the Russians would develop it. Well, they sure did, but it was obvious that there would be no security. And I think it is obvious now that weapons are compeltely out of proportion, that they no longer have any function of foreign policy."

Even if the bomb served little purpose in foreign affaris, however, there was a tendency to reach for it—to use it as a threat when things were going badly. On November 30, 1950, for instance, while American troops in Korea were being pushed back by the Chinese, President Truman told a press conference that the United States did not rule out the use of nuclear bombs. Coming three months after a call by Secretary of the Navy Francis P. Matthews for a preventative war, the announcement disturbed America's allies.

Prime Minister Clement Attlee of Great Britain hastened to Washington to express his concern. It was not likely that the Soviet Union and China would stand by while North Korea was being bombed out of existence. Once the "fire-break" between conventional war and nuclear war was breached, hostilities were destined to enlarge, and if they did, the Soviet Union might overrun all of Western Europe.

As luck would have it, on the third day of Attlee's visit the Pentagon's early-warning radar system indicated that Russian planes were headed southeast on a course that could bring them over Washington in two to three hours. The American military machine was put on a war alert. Fortunately, by the time Attlee and Secretary of State Dean Acheson reached the White House, the unidentified objects disappeared from the radar screen. The Pentagon's guess was that what on the radar screen had looked like enemy planes were probably nothing but a flock of geese.

Truman reassured Atlee that he wasn't thinking of using nuclear bombs in Korea. His press comments, he said, were merely a means of putting pressure on the Communists.

But the atomic issue came up again in 1953. The war had been indecisive. Though North Korea had only 9 million inhabitants, as against 21 million for South Korea, its armies overran three quarters of the South within a few weeks. It was only when the United States became involved, that General MacArthur's troops were able, in September 1950, to recapture the South Korean capital, Seoul. A month later United States forces took the North Korean capital, Pyongyang, and were advancing toward the Yalu River, which formed the border with China.

At this point, however, the Chinese sent 320,000 "volunteers" into the fray. Within three weeks the American armies were pushed back 300 miles, and 105,000 troops had to be evacuated by the U.S. Navy. The United States regained lost ground after a while, but the war had become a stalemate, with neither side capable of defeating the other. In July 1951, three months after MacArthur had been relieved of his command, negotiations began for an armistice. Unfortunately the talks continued fruitlessly for a year and a half. By that time Truman had left office, and General Dwight D. ("Ike") Eisenhower had been elected President. One of the promises Ike had made during the campaign was that he would end the war.

That was easier said than done, however. Some officials favored a new military offensive. In his memoirs Eisenhower tells us that if the United States were to mount such an offensive, "it was clear that we would have to use atomic weapons. This necessity was suggested to me by General MacArthur. . . . But an American decision to use them at that time would have created strong disrupting feelings between ourselves and our allies." There were also "other problems, not the least of which would be the possibility of the Soviet Union entering the war. . . . We knew that the Soviets had atomic weapons in quantity, and estimated that they would soon explode a hydrogen device. Of all the Asian targets which might be subjected to Soviet bombing, I was most concerned about the unprotected cities of Japan."

Eisenhower spread the word through intermediaries that the United States was thinking of using atomic weapons. "I let it be known," he later revealed, "that if there was not going to be an armistice . . . we were not going to be bound by the kind of weapons that we would use. . . . I don't mean to say that we'd have used those great big things and destroyed cities, but we would use them enough to win and we, of course, would have tried to keep them on military targets, not civil targets."

Fortunately for all concerned, an armistice was finally signed on July 27, 1953.

"Reaching for the bomb," however, became almost a reflex for some American officials. A year after the Korean War ended, Major General Charles A. Willoughby, a former aide to General MacArthur, proposed that the United States use atom and hydrogen bombs to blast "a belt of scorched earth" across the Communists' path in Asia. Government leaders did not adopt the Willoughby plan, but it is a good bet that the general and others who shared his military philosophy continued to favor a nuclear "belt of scorched earth."

The bomb was an immensely powerful weapon, but it wasn't always clear what one could do with it. This confusion was reflected in strategic policy. During the Truman administration, Secretary Stimson and three other Cabinet members called for "atomic partnership" with the Soviet Union, in order to avoid an arms race. At the opposite end of the spectrum, such men as General Orville Anderson and Secretary of the Navy Francis Matthews urged "preventative war." President Truman's position— "containment" —was to prepare for nuclear war, but concentrate on economic and political pressures that might force the Soviets to change their system.

The official strategy of the Eisenhower administration was called "massive retaliation." Secretary of State John Foster Dulles announced this policy six months after the end of the Korean War. As a private citizen in March 1949 he had told *U.S. News & World Report* that he did "not know any responsible official, military or civilian, in this government or any government, who believes that the Soviet government plans conquest by open military aggression." But as Secretary of State he wanted to punctuate American "toughness" and "determination." Should there be a new aggression like Korea, he said, the Eisenhower administration would retaliate instantly and with all its power. The Kremlin was advised, in effect, that if its armies went beyond the borders of the Communist world, it would be wiped out.

"Massive retaliation" sounded awesome—and feasible. The general estimate in 1953–54 was that the Pentagon had thousands of nuclear warheads, the Soviets only three hundred. With this lopsided ratio the United States should be able to win. Yet the other side of the equation was that America would have to pay a fearsome price. If only a few Soviet bombers could get through American defenses, the cost in lives would be appalling. A 1953 series of articles in *Fortune* magazine calculated that American interceptor planes and antiaircraft artillery could bring down fifteen or twenty of every hundred attacking Soviet bombers, but the other 80 or 85 would get through. If the raid took place at night, 99 out of 100 would get through. If the Soviets could drop 250 H-bombs on American cities, it would cause 70 million deaths, plus injuries for many millions more. Of course Russia, too, would be devastated, but that was small comfort.

The strategy of massive retaliation was never more than a bluff. In 1954 the Viet Minh—Communist guerrillas in Vietnam—surrounded French troops at Dienbienphu, and were on the verge of annihilating them. To prevent a fiasco, Dulles offered atomic weapons to France. One or more nuclear bombs would be dropped on China, near the Indochina border. Two would be used against the Viet Minh at Dienbienphu. The French never accepted the offer; they were defeated and forced out of Vietnam. Despite Dulles' policy of massive retaliation, however, no nuclear bombs were launched by the United States against China, the Soviet Union, or the Viet Minh.

Two years later there was a revolt by students and workers against the Communist government of Hungary. Soviet troops put down the uprising. Theoretically, this was the kind of occasion that called for massive retaliation by the United States.

Eisenhower and Dulles, however, never considered such action; it was too risky.

Understandably, then, the thought occurred to some foreign-policy leaders that massive retaliation was not workable. As one expert put it: "The more powerful the weapons, the greater the reluctance to use them." A policy of massive retaliation left the United States with only a single option—to fight a major war even if the dispute was over a relatively minor issue. Suppose, for instance, that China were to seize two islands near its mainland, Quemoy and Matsu. Was it worthwhile to start World War III in order to reclaim them, or should lesser measures be taken?

The Council on Foreign Relations assembled thirty-four prominent business, government, and academic leaders to study the question. The project director was a thirty-four-year-old German emigré who had only recently received his Ph.D. from Harvard, Henry Kissinger. After a year and a half the group's conclusions were distilled by Kissinger into a book, *Nuclear Weapons and Foreign Policy,* which became an instant best seller. The focus of American strategy, it said, should not be on massive retaliation but on limited war.

"Limited war," wrote Kissinger, "has become the form of conflict which enables us to derive the greatest strategic advantage. . . ." Any "aggression" by the Soviet bloc would still "be resisted with nuclear weapons," but "we should make every effort to limit their effect and to spare the civilian population."

In Kissinger's scenario the United States would announce that it would use no more than 500 kilotons of explosive power (equal to about 40 Hiroshima bombs). The attack would be limited to a small area—say, 500 miles—and would avoid cities. Both sides would fight a restrained war with tactical nuclear weapons such as the Davy Crockett (a bazooka missile), the Long John (with a 10-mile range), the Corporal and Sergeant

(75-mile range), and the Pershing (500-mile range). The fighting would go on, presumably, until one or the other side decided to give up.

There was something artificial about Kissinger's scenario. It assumed the Russians could be persuaded by the United States to end the conflict after they had dropped 500 kilotons on American lines. Edward Teller went further. He foresaw a time when limited wars could be fought "in a humane way." This could be done, he said, by producing "clean" hydrogen bombs —bombs that caused little radioactive fallout. Thus one category of victims would be saved—those who might die of radioactivity. Blast and fire, of course, would continue to take their toll.

The question asked by many was: Could a limited nuclear war stay limited? In a 1961 article titled "A Reappraisal," Kissinger himself conceded that it wasn't likely. George F. Kennan, a scholar and diplomat, disparaged the idea that you could come to an understanding with an enemy to restrict military action. In his book *Russia, the Atom, and the West* he called it "a very slender and wishful hope indeed." R.M.S. Blackett, a British Nobel prize winner, concluded that Kissinger's scenario for limited nuclear war was "plain poppycock—and very dangerous."

Moreover, what the United States and the Soviet Union might call a "limited" exchange would be total for some of their allies. Two war games conducted by the Pentagon in Louisiana and Europe in 1955 made this abundantly clear. In one of these games, Operation Carte Blanche, 335 bombs were "dropped" on West Germany. The game indicated that 5.2 million of Germany's 49 million people would be dead or wounded within two days. If the war lasted as much as three weeks, there would be few healthy people left in Germany— and not many doctors or hospitals to care for them.

The limited-war strategy, like massive retaliation, obviously posed many problems. Nonetheless the technology for limited war was already at hand. In the summer of 1948, long before Kissinger wrote his book, a group of scientists held a series of conferences in California on the uses of nuclear weapons. One of the conclusions of this Project Vista was that the United States should begin making "small" nuclear weapons for "local warfare"—as small perhaps as one tenth of a kiloton (equivalent to 100 tons of TNT). A series of tests in 1951 showed that sub-kiloton bombs indeed were practical. Technology thus played a hand in formulating strategy. The nation's leaders were less timid about using "small" weapons over a limited area than they might have been about weapons that would destroy an average city.

There were at least seven occasions during the 1950's and 1960's when the United States government seriously considered limited nuclear war. Two have already been noted—Eisenhower's plan to end the Korean War with an atomic attack, and the offer of nuclear weapons to France when it was besieged at Dienbienphu. We will come to the others presently.

Fortunately, actual nuclear engagement was avoided in each instance. On the other hand, there was no disarmament either. President Truman's Baruch Plan of 1946 provided that "manufacture of atomic bombs shall stop" and "existing bombs shall be disposed of. . . ." President Eisenhower, in his address to the United Nations (December 8, 1953), called on the superpowers to "begin to diminish the potential destructive power of the world's atomic stockpiles." He urged a program of "atomic power for peace" —using the atom for generating electricity instead of for making bombs.

Still, all efforts to negotiate a disarmament pact in the first decade of the nuclear age failed. The Baruch Plan was rejected by the Soviets on the grounds that it had "jokers" that would allow the United States to continue making atomic weapons, whereas the Soviet Union would have to stop its research and development immediately. Talks continued for a while, but by 1948 an impasse had been reached. In 1949, of course, a new factor was added to the equation—the Soviets had exploded their own bomb. And in 1950, with the Korean War under way, disarmament talks languished.

The most promising opportunity for nuclear disarmament occurred in 1954–55. The long-time Soviet leader, Joseph Stalin, had died in March 1953, and his successor, Georgi Malenkov, seemed to be more flexible and moderate. Public opinion everywhere again demanded that the bomb be shelved. The war in Korea was over, and Eisenhower had proclaimed that now, with both powers having the H-bomb, there was "no longer any alternative to peace."

In the wake of these developments Britain and France put forth a plan to break the impasse in May 1954. Their proposal sketched step by step how the arms race would be de-escalated. The first step would prohibit use of nuclear weapons "except for defense against aggression." The next step would be for the United States, the Soviet Union, and China to reduce their conventional forces to a million or a million and a half troops each (Britain and France would trim theirs to 650,000 each). When the first half of the conventional arms scale-down was completed and controls had been set up, the superpowers would stop producing nuclear weapons.

Moscow agreed to this plan as a "basis for talks," and on May 10, 1955, surprised the whole world by introducing a draft treaty that virtually accepted the British-French scheme. Nobel prize winner Philip Noel-Baker called this the "moment of hope." French leader Jules Moch stated that "the whole thing looks too good to be true." The United States delegate to the disarmament talks said he was "gratified" that Moscow had finally accepted "in large measure" concepts "which we have put forward over a considerable period of time."

But at this juncture the United States astonished the world by rejecting the West's own proposal. Instead, Washington suggested a scheme for "open skies": the United States and the U.S.S.R. would fly over each other's territory, at will, to map military installations. The Russians rejected the idea as "nothing more than a bald espionage plot." There would be a lot of inspection of each side's territory, but no disarmament. A month later Harold Stassen, the United States delegate, officially withdrew the previous proposals.

"For years," commented journalist I.F. Stone, "we had accused the Russians of proposing disarmament without inspection. Now it looked as if we were proposing inspection without disarmament."

If there was no nuclear war in the 1950's, there were also no effective checks on the nuclear arms race.

5. NO WINNERS

"WAR HAS BECOME A FRANKENSTEIN TO DESTROY BOTH SIDES. . . .
NO LONGER DOES IT POSSESS THE CHANCE OF THE WINNER OF THE
DUEL—IT CONTAINS, RATHER, THE GERMS OF DOUBLE SUICIDE."
General Douglas MacArthur

The first task of the United States in the nuclear age was to produce the weapon itself, the bomb. The second was to find a means of delivering it. When Albert Einstein wrote Roosevelt in August 1939 urging a nuclear program, he warned that an atomic bomb would be "too heavy for transportation by air." It would have to be delivered, he thought, by boat—and exploded in the enemy's port. It wasn't because the nuclear fuel weighed so much—the uranium or plutonium needed for an atomic bomb came to only 10 pounds and could be contained in a baseball or softball. But there was a considerable amount of chemical explosive and other equipment that went into the weapon, making it large and unwieldy.

Einstein, however, proved to be wrong. The Hiroshima and Nagasaki bombs were delivered to their targets by airplanes. During the first decade of the nuclear age, therefore, the United States concentrated on bombers. It developed a long-range plane, the B-52, and a medium-range one, the B-47.

But from the very beginning military leaders sought a less

51

vulnerable means of delivery. A bomber could be destroyed by enemy bombs while parked on the airfield or by antiaircraft guns as it approached its target. It was also relatively "slow" —a few hundred miles an hour.

One possibility considered was a missile like the one Hitler's engineers had built at the end of World War II. The V-2, however, was a single-stage rocket with a range of only 200 miles. And it wasn't particularly accurate; sometimes it missed its target in Britain by 15 or 20 miles. The V-2 didn't seem to be the answer.

The Soviet explosion of an H-bomb and development of a long-range bomber made American strategists edgy. The United States, many of them said, was about to lose its nuclear superiority. In the mid-1950's military spokesmen and the CIA began talking of a "bomber gap." By the end of the decade, they said, the Soviet Union would have twice as many long-range bombers as the United States, and they urged President Eisenhower to increase spending for the B-52 program. It turned out that these estimates were far from the mark—a point that President Eisenhower made in his last State of the Union address. "The bomber gap of several years ago," said the President on January 12, 1961, "was always a fiction." The United States then had 600 B-52 and 1,400 B-47 bomber planes; the Soviets had nowhere near that number, it is now admitted.

Nevertheless there was a renewed interest in the missile during the 1950's. Encouraged by mathematician John von Neumann, the Air Force decided to take another try at it. This time it succeeded.

By mid-1957, the scientists and engineers began providing the Pentagon with one new generation of ballistic missiles after another. A ballistic missile has a high trajectory, being propelled by a rocket into the atmosphere, from there into the stratosphere, then back again into the atmosphere. The first ballistic missile—the Atlas—was a two-stage vehicle, with three rocket engines, fueled by liquid oxygen and kerosene. It was 85 feet long, weighed 120 tons, and was accurate within five miles of its target—later, two miles, then one mile. By 1962 the Pentagon had produced 126 Atlas ICBMs (intercontinental ballistic missiles).

Next came the Titan and Titan II, also liquid-fueled, but with slightly more thrust—430,000 pounds. Titan II was 110 feet long and weighed 125 tons. Still later the Minuteman came off the assembly line. This missile was shorter and lighter. It was 54 feet in length and 33 tons in weight, fitting a silo only 10 feet in diameter and 80 feet deep. It had a range of 6,000 miles, and unlike the other two missiles, it had the additional advantage that it used a *solid* fuel. As of this writing there are in United States silos one thousand Minutemen and fifty-four Titans (less two that blew up in Arkansas and Kansas.) A new missile, the MX (missile experimental), is also under development and is expected to be deployed by the late 1980's. Technologically it will be a great improvement over the Minuteman. It will carry ten warheads and will be able to hit a target 8,000 miles away within 100 to 300 feet.

In addition it can be *mobile.* Instead of being emplaced in individual silos, the 200 MX can be constantly hauled from one shelter to another, so that the Soviets will never know where they are. All told, there were to be 4,600 shelters, an average of 23 per missile—until President Reagan modified the plan in 1981. The original cost estimate by the Pentagon was put at $34 billion, but is expected to run two or three times that amount.

People in Nevada and Utah objected that their water supply would be used up and their whole way of life adversely changed if the MXs were to be placed in their area. Former CIA Director

Stansfield Turner added another objection, namely, that the Russians could cancel the advantage of mobility simply by deploying another 4,600 warheads on their big missiles.

The missile changed the nature of nuclear strategy. In war, as in football, there is offense and defense. A bomber is an offensive weapon, an antiaircraft gun defends against the bomber by shooting it down. From the very beginning of the nuclear age strategists were conscious of the lopsided relationship between offense and defense. A bomber that pierced antiaircraft defenses in the *pre*-nuclear age could destroy a square block or a half block. If you shot down 10 of every 100 bombers in each raid, you would eventually make it too costly for the enemy to continue his raids. But a bomber that pierced antiaircraft defenses in the nuclear age could destroy a whole city, or most of it. Atom and hydrogen bombs could wreak hundreds of times more damage than any warheads ever devised. Even if you could shoot down 90 of every 100 bombers the offense would have achieved its objective. Defense would be little more than an irritant.

Back in 1945 James Franck of the University of Chicago had warned the Truman administration that science was not likely to develop a defense against "new weapons of aggression." The missile tilted the odds even further against defense. For although it was possible to shoot down *some* bombers flying at 400–500 miles an hour, there was no antiaircraft gun or fighter plane that could bring down a pilotless missile moving at 9,400 miles an hour. Thus the superpowers were reaching the stage where the United States would be able to destroy the Soviet Union, and the Soviet Union would be able to destroy the United States—and neither country could do anything to prevent it. There was no defense. Nuclear war was becoming unwinnable.

Tilting the scale even more in favor of offense in the nuclear age was the development of rockets for submarines. In 1956 the Navy began work on a solid-fuel rocket, and in a few years it produced the Polaris. Only 28½ feet long, it was fitted with a 600-pound warhead that packed two thirds of a megaton explosive power—50 times as much as the Hiroshima bomb. In a sense this was more sensational than the Air Force's missile because the Polaris could be fired from a moving submarine undersea and would have a range of 1,200 nautical miles.

Moreover, the Polaris submarine—companion to the Polaris missile—was also nuclear-fueled and could stay underwater far longer than any previous sub. In the terminology of strategists, it was "invulnerable." It was next to impossible for an enemy to locate it and destroy it. Even if the Soviets could "kill" every one of America's 1,054 land-based missiles and every bomber in Europe and Asia, the 41 nuclear submarines could still annihilate every major Soviet city.

In subsequent years the Navy developed a more sophisticated missile, the Poseidon, which could carry 10–14 warheads, each aimed at a different target. Work is presently nearing completion on the Trident submarine and the Trident missile, which carries 8 warheads and can hit a target 4,000 miles away. The first ones are now being deployed.

The Russians were making similar strides in technology, though always a little behind the United States. It had taken them four years to catch up with the atom bomb, but only nine months to catch up with the hydrogen bomb. In one or two respects they were ahead of the United States. For instance, on October 4, 1957, the Soviets launched the first space vehicle ever to orbit the earth. It made history and caused concern in Washington that the Russians might be getting ahead of the United States. Certainly that was true as far as *thrust* (power, or forward motion) was concerned. That first satellite, Sputnik, had enough thrust to carry a payload of half a ton. The second and third Sputniks had rockets with a thrust of 800,000 pounds —twice that of America's Atlas missile. Generally the United States was ahead both in originating new weapons and in their sophistication. But it didn't matter too much anymore because it was becoming evident that neither superpower could get so far ahead that it would have an *absolute* advantage—the ability to win. What one nation could produce today, the other could produce soon thereafter.

As the missile age began, it became apparent to experts that no matter what each side did, the cost in life and property of a full-scale nuclear war was growing almost by geometric progression. In May 1956, General Earle Partridge told a congressional subcommittee that 50 nuclear bombs would bring under fire 40 percent of the Soviet population and 60 percent of its industry. The National Planning Association in a study two years later concluded that 200 warheads were enough to demolish "a large nation state." By this time, of course, both superpowers had many times that number.

The mad momentum of technology caused grave dismay in many places during the 1950's. Where would it end? Secretary of the Air Force Donald A. Quarles wrote an article for *Air Force Magazine* asking, "How much is enough?"

"The buildup of atomic power" he said, "makes total war an unthinkable catastrophe for both sides." It was time to start thinking of how to end the arms race rather than increasing the tempo of rearmament. Many people felt that way, because a movement of sorts sprang up in opposition to the arms race. It didn't center around the missile but around the warhead— more specifically, around the issue of radioactivity resulting from nuclear testing.

An early cause of concern was the knowledge that during the hydrogen-bomb test at Bikini in 1954, hundreds of Marshall

Islanders escaped death from radioactive fallout only because of favorable winds. Some, however, did die. Twenty-three Japanese fishermen were equally unfortunate, as the fallout spread over 7,000 square miles and made them deathly sick.

Soon scientists, political leaders, and peace groups began to focus attention on nuclear testing. A secret Atomic Energy Committee study in 1953 (made public five years later) indicated that one of the by-products of testing was a radioactive substance called strontium 90. Its radioactivity lasts for many years, tends to penetrate bone, and causes cancer. AEC experts concluded that after each test, strontium 90 made its way around the world—through the stratosphere—to lodge in vegetables and milk. This was particularly dangerous for children. Another worrisome by-product of nuclear testing was iodine 131, which also contaminates milk and can cause thyroid cancer, especially in children. There were other hazardous substances in radioactive fallout—cesium 137, plutonium 239 (which still is somewhat radioactive after 250,000 years), and others.

The distressing feature about this radioactivity is that it usually doesn't take its toll at once. The cancer might not appear for ten, twenty, or thirty years. Some people who were subjected to radioactivity from nuclear testing in Utah and Nevada during the 1950's, for instance, died of cancer late in the 1970's —and are still dying of it.

A formal request to suspend nuclear testing was made by India's prime minister, Jawaharlal Nehru, a month after the nearly disastrous Bikini test in 1954. Nehru's appeal brought no action. A little later a conference of Third World nations made another demand on the superpowers, and repeated it in 1955. In May 1955 the Soviet Union included a ban on testing as part of its disarmament plan.

Two years later the Soviets made a separate proposal for a

test ban— "if only for a period of two or three years." The offer called for inspection posts in the Soviet Union, the United States, Britain, and the Pacific Ocean area, to see if anyone was cheating. Britain was included because it had joined the nuclear club in October 2, 1952, when it exploded its first atomic device. Unfortunately the argument over how many control posts there should be—and how many inspections—continued on and on. The Soviets wanted fewer, the United States more.

Nonetheless there was another one of those "moments of hope" toward the end of the decade. Dr. Linus Pauling, the American scientist who would later win two Nobel prizes, circulated a petition to scientists around the world calling for "an international agreement to stop the testing of nuclear bombs." It was signed by nine thousand scientists in forty-three countries and presented to the United Nations Secretary-General in January 1958. Public opinion, not only abroad but here, was turning around.

In April 1958 the Soviet leader Nikita Khrushchev announced a unilateral cessation of tests—without waiting for an agreement with the United States to do likewise. The Soviet leader, however, publicly urged President Eisenhower to follow suit. Washington held off for a while. It repeated old arguments that there must be "adequate inspection," but a few months later declared its own suspension of tests. In a display of what could be done with good faith, the two superpowers abstained from testing for more than two years—until the Soviets resumed in September 1961.

Meanwhile negotiations began for a formal test ban treaty. They lasted from April 18, 1961—three months after John F. Kennedy became President—to August 5, 1963. Holding up agreement was a familiar dispute: How many inspections should each side be allowed of the other side's territory? The Soviet Union wanted two or three a year, the United States, twelve to twenty-one. Many scientists insisted the argument was irrelevant because there were adequate means for detecting a nuclear test through seismology—similar to the way earthquakes are detected. Finally an agreement was reached and duly signed by 106 nations. Significantly, France (which tested its first bomb in 1960), and China (which was preparing its first test) refused to sign. The treaty banned tests in the atmosphere, outer space, and underwater—but not underground.

The loophole permitting underground testing seriously eroded the value of the treaty. The Russians and a top American negotiator, Adrian Fisher, had urged a complete test ban —underground as well as in the atmosphere. But in a confidential memorandum the Pentagon prevailed on President Kennedy to allow it a "safeguard." The Joint Chiefs of Staff said that such tests were vital to "improve our weapons." From their viewpoint the Joint Chiefs were right, of course, for if *all* tests had been banned, it would have been next to impossible to develop the complex weapons conceived by scientists and engineers in the ensuing years. It would have ended or severely slowed down the nuclear arms race. But Kennedy ruled with the military on this issue, and the final pact was seriously flawed.

The practical result was that testing not only continued—in large underground cavities—but increased in numbers. In the nineteen years from 1945 through 1963, the Soviets had conducted 164 tests and the United States 282 tests—an average of 23 a year. But in the ten years from August 1963 to June 1973, the Soviets carried out 121 underground tests and the United States 259—an average of 38 a year.

The march of technology was unchecked through the 1950's —it proceeded from atom bombs to hydrogen bombs to small "tactical" bombs to missiles to nuclear submarines. But efforts at disarmament, as already noted, ran into obstacles. From 1950 to 1953, there were the tensions of the Korean War. In 1956 the Soviets protested the war by Britain, France, and Israel against Egypt, whereas the United States and its allies protested with equal vigor against the Soviet suppression of a popular revolt in Hungary. In 1957, after the Russians launched Sputnik, American sights were set on the space race rather than on disarmament.

Then, in 1958, there was a crisis over two tiny islands in China, Quemoy and Matsu. Chiang Kai-shek's Formosa troops were stationed in these two fortresses on the Chinese mainland, and Chinese Communist troops were trying to dislodge them. The American Joint Chiefs advised President Eisenhower that the islands could not be held unless the United States was prepared to drop nuclear bombs on China. In fact, the National Security Council tentatively approved this step. Fortunately, it was never taken.

That year, too, there was another Cold War crisis—this time over Berlin. Premier Khrushchev announced in November that the Soviet Union was ready to turn over East Berlin to East Germany. Hitherto it had been under Soviet control. If it should pass to other hands, American officials would have to renegotiate the right of access to West Berlin, which was totally surrounded by East Germany. The only way to get there, other than by air, was through a "corridor" controlled by the Soviet Union—and soon, presumably, by East Germany.

Tensions abated somewhat after Khrushchev visited President Eisenhower at Camp David in late 1959. The Soviet premier withdrew his threat concerning Berlin, and the two heads of state scheduled a summit meeting for Paris the following May. Hopes were raised everywhere that at last the two leaders would take serious steps toward disarmament.

But on May 1, 1960, an American U-2 spy plane, packed with

photographic equipment, was shot down 1,300 miles inside Soviet territory. When Khrushchev announced the incident, Eisenhower first said that the pilot was on a meteorological mission—gathering weather information—and had lost his way. It wasn't a very good explanation. Few people believed that a pilot could lose his way for 1,300 miles. Eisenhower may have thought that the pilot—Gary Powers—had perished in the accident and therefore could not contradict him. But in fact the pilot had parachuted, been captured by the Soviets, and had admitted he had been spying.

When this became known, Eisenhower conceded the spy mission, but claimed the United States had a *right* to fly over Soviet territory. One thing led to another, and the summit meeting was called off.

Another turn toward peace had been aborted.

The representative of Cuba to the United Nations, Dr. Mario Garcia-Inchaustegui, addresses the United Nations Security Council during the October Missile Crisis in 1962.

The nuclear blast of an antisubmarine rocket missile

A Soviet SS-9 intercontinental ballistic missile

Ambassadors Charles C. Stelle of the United States and Semyon K. Tsarapkin of the Soviet Union sign an agreement in Geneva, Switzerland, establishing a "hot line" between Washington, D.C., and Moscow in June 1963.

Left: A Trident missile is launched. The Trident carries eight warheads and can hit a target 4,000 miles away.

U.S. NAVY

Right: An experimental nuclear reactor in Trombay, India

UNITED NATIONS

Mushroom cloud formed over an uninhabited island in the Pacific after an explosion of an atomic bomb by France

UNITED NATIONS / PHOTO BY SYGMA

A protester at the University of California Livermore Laboratory

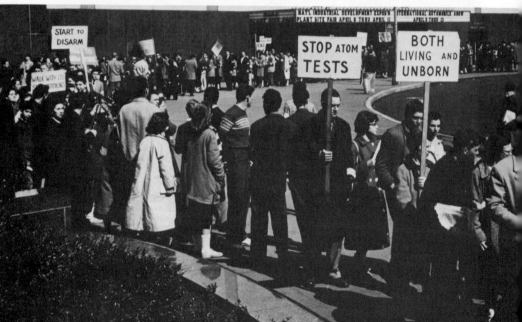

Top: A child hands "Peace Book" to Disarmament Committee Chairman François de la Gorce in Geneva in February 1981.   UNITED NATIONS

Bottom: Walk for Peace in New York City, Easter, 1958   WAR RESISTERS LEAGUE

Top: Continental Walk for Disarmament and Social Justice Rally in Washington, D.C., on October 16, 1976   KARL BISSINGER, WAR RESISTERS LEAGUE

Bottom: Demonstration against the neutron bomb in New York City on August 13, 1981
GRACE HEDEMANN, WAR RESISTERS LEAGUE

6. PREPARE FOR EVERYTHING

"IF WE THINK WE ARE GOING TO GET SECURITY BY MILITARY STRENGTH, WE ARE WRONG." General Alfred M. Gruenther

There was an expectation of major change when John F. Kennedy was sworn in as the 35th President on January 20, 1961. Kennedy—or JFK, as he was often called—was the first and only Catholic to attain this high office. He was young, handsome, charismatic, and he used language that appealed to young idealists. "Ask not what your country can do for you," he said in his inaugural address. "Ask what you can do for your country." In another portion of the speech he said: "If a free society cannot help the many who are poor, it cannot save the few who are rich."

Kennedy read books and wrote books. In one of them, *The Strategy of Peace,* he expressed the view that limited nuclear wars had little chance to remain limited: "Inevitably the use of small nuclear armaments will lead to larger nuclear armaments on both sides, until the world-wide holocaust has begun." In a speech to the United Nations, after becoming President, he warned that "mankind must put an end to war or war will put an end to mankind."

Even Kennedy, however, did not put an end to the nuclear race. He rejected the Dulles Doctrine of massive retaliation. But he continued the atomic buildup.

During the election campaign Kennedy made much ado about something called the "missile gap." The Russians, he said, were acquiring missiles so rapidly that by the early 1960's they would have three times as many as the United States. As it turned out, there never was a missile gap, just as there hadn't been a "bomber gap" in 1956. Instead of 600 to 800 missiles, as claimed by the Air Force, the Soviets had only 50 to 100.

Nonetheless, Kennedy enlarged the arsenal of missiles and bombs. At his request Congress authorized a supplementary expenditure of $1.2 billion for the Polaris and Minuteman missile programs. The climb continued throughout the Kennedy and into the Johnson administrations. Within five years the American delivery system reached a peak of 1,054 land-based intercontinental ballistic missiles (ICBMs), 656 submarine-launched ballistic missiles (SLBMs), and 630 B-52 bombers.

Perhaps the most curious nuclear development in the Kennedy years was the fallout shelter program. It dated back to 1960, when the Pentagon held a top-secret meeting of a dozen influential people, including Governor Nelson Rockefeller of New York. Their conclusion was that the State Department needed "muscle" for negotiations with the Soviet Union. Unless the United States proved it was ready to wage a nuclear war, the Russians might not take it seriously. Fallout shelters would convince the Soviets that Americans meant business.

Kennedy was not enthusiastic about this proposal, but he decided to move with the tide. Americans were asked to build shelters in their backyards or in their basements to protect them from radiation in case of nuclear war. U.S. Steel marketed a $1,800 prefabricated shelter capable of shielding six persons.

General Mills marketed a new food called MPF, Multi-Purpose Food, for those cooped up in shelters. A National Shelter Association was formed by manufacturers, and its president predicted that 1,000 companies would ultimately build $200 billion worth of shelters. *Life* magazine, then the second most widely read publication in the United States, predicted that with fallout shelters, "97 out of 100 people can be saved."

Americans did not believe it. They had a subliminal feeling that if nuclear war came, there really was no defense. It made no sense, therefore, to invest hundreds or thousands of dollars in something that would be useless. A vast majority of Americans failed to respond to Kennedy's plea. Even government officials who proposed the plan did nothing to build shelters for themselves. The project died almost at birth, and it was never revived.

But if the shelter program was a dud, Kennedy clearly did not pull back from the nuclear commitment of his predecessors. What he did was add another dimension to American strategy: a program for dealing with "insurgency." Since World War II dozens of former colonies had broken away from the British, French, and other powers—just as the United States itself had done in 1776. Some turned to the Soviet Union for support—China, for instance, and others, such as Tunisia, to the United States. Still others were "neutralist"— friendly to both sides, or to neither, like India.

As the old colonial order disintegrated, the United States tried to win "Third World" nations to the Western banner. Sometimes the Central Intelligence Agency secretly intervened to remove a government Washington didn't like—or to put one in that Washington did like. Thus in 1953–54, the CIA financed a revolt against the regime of Jacobo Arbenz in Guatemala. Arbenz was considered neutralist or pro-Soviet. At about the same time the CIA organized a coup d'etat to remove Prime Minister Mohammed Mossadegh of Iran and return to power the exiled Shah. During a revolution in Lebanon in 1957, 10,000 United States troops were put ashore in the Lebanese capital, Beirut, in support of the conservative forces in that country.

Kennedy felt that the worldwide social turbulence was America's most immediate security problem. And he attributed a good part of this unrest to the Soviet Union. "We face a relentless struggle in every corner of the globe," the President told newspaper editors in April 1961. That struggle "goes far beyond the clash of armies, or even nuclear weapons. The armies are there, and in large number. The nuclear armaments are there. But they serve primarily as the shield behind which subversion, infiltration, and a host of other tactics steadily advance. . . ." The main immediate danger to the West, in other words, was not nuclear war but revolutions in Asia, Africa, and Latin America.

To meet this challenge the Kennedy team developed a new strategy called "graduated response," or "flexible response." Instead of putting their eggs almost entirely in the nuclear basket, they decided to strengthen all aspects of the military machine. "Graduated response" meant that the President would have a grab bag of options, ranging from CIA activity to small conventional wars to big nuclear wars. "Flexible response" meant to be prepared for everything. Ultimately the buildup was so extensive that the Pentagon claimed it was capable of fighting "two and a half wars" at once—a NATO war in Europe, a war in Asia against China, and a minor war in Latin America with a small nation like the Dominican Republic.

This was a big change from the Eisenhower and Dulles strategy. The Pentagon was still ready to fight a nuclear war, but under General Maxwell Taylor's prodding, its *active* concern was counterinsurgency—fighting "little wars," either against guerrillas or against a developing country.

The first test of the "little war" strategy came in Cuba. The crisis dated back to December 1956, when a young Havana lawyer named Fidel Castro had led a small band of eighty-two revolutionaries against the United States–supported regime of Fulgencio Batista. Landing from Mexico aboard an over-crowded 58-foot yacht, the eighty-two were cut down to a mere dozen before they reached the mountains. Nonetheless they eventually amassed a force of 1,200 men and defeated Batista's army of 43,000. Castro came to power on New Year's Day 1959.

United States relations with Castro went from bad to worse, particularly after the new government nationalized ranches and sugar lands owned by United States companies. During the next two years, planes based in Florida, operated by Cuban exiles hostile to Castro, bombed Cuba repeatedly. In March 1960 they blew up a French ship in the Havana harbor, killing 75 and injuring 300. All of this was forerunner to a planned invasion of Cuba by an exile force, trained and organized by the CIA.

The decision to undertake this project was made by Eisenhower, on recommendation by his Vice-President, Richard Nixon. But Kennedy carried out the plan. In April 1961 four cargo ships and a dozen smaller crafts, carrying 1,400 exiles, approached Playa Larga, Playa Giron, and Bahia de Cochinos (Bay of Pigs) on Cuba's southern shore. They were accompanied by United States destroyers. Castro's forces, however, were ready for them. They blew up the exiles' ammunition ship and many B-26 planes. The would-be invaders failed to take a single objective or spark a single revolt within the Cuban population. Their Operation Pluto, which had taken thirteen months to prepare and had cost the United States $45 million, collapsed within three days.

Eighteen months after this debacle, there was a sequel that brought the Soviet Union and the United States within a hair of all-out nuclear war. The friction between the United States and Cuba continued. An embargo was placed on shipping—everything but food and medicine—to the island. The exiles, meanwhile, continued their raids on Cuba, using United States ports as a base.

According to Soviet and Fidelista sources, the two Communist countries concluded that a second invasion of Cuba was imminent. Their fears were reinforced by a speech made by Defense Secretary Robert S. McNamara, which led Khrushchev to believe that the United States was preparing a surprise attack on the Soviet Union itself.

In a commencement address at Ann Arbor, Michigan, on June 16, 1962, the Secretary outlined a strategy for "counterforce." America's "principal military objectives," he said, "should be the destruction of the enemy's military forces, not his civilian population." Instead of a "counter-city" strategy that would kill millions of people, the Pentagon would concentrate on destroying Russia's bombers and missiles.

This sounded humane: instead of killing people, the United States would "kill" missile silos. But in fact the policy was more dangerous. Counterforce meant a surprise attack—a "first strike." The reason is obvious. It makes no sense to hit the enemy's missile silos if their missiles have already been launched—if they are no longer there. In that case, United States missiles would hit only empty holes. The only reason for a counterforce strategy was to strike first, to take the enemy by surprise, while his missiles were still in their silos.

Nikita Khrushchev denounced McNamara's speech as "a camouflage for nuclear war," and took out ads in American newspapers warning that Washington was "preparing for a nuclear war."

In the face of what they considered a twin threat, Khrushchev and Castro secretly emplaced a couple of dozen intermediate-range missiles in Cuba. Although U-2 flights over Cuba indicated that something strange was going on, the Soviet Ambassador to Washington assured Robert Kennedy that weapons sent to the island were only for "defensive" purposes. In October, however, new information secured from overflights by American planes convinced President Kennedy beyond doubt that ballistic missiles were being stationed in San Cristobal, Cuba.

The President's response showed he was prepared to go all the way to nuclear confrontation. Crews of 144 intercontinental ballistic missiles were put on special alert in the United States. The Navy deployed 183 ships, with 110,000 men aboard, around Cuba. In addition, 1,000 planes were put "on the ready," and 100,000 troops (with 200,000 more available if needed) were poised to invade the island.

This show of strength became known in history as the "October Missile Crisis." One of its unique features was that the President acted entirely on his own. No effort was made to call Congress into session to vote on whether the President should be given the right to make war. A special "Executive Committee" (Ex Com) was established to consider three alternatives: do nothing, blockade Cuba—as a first step, or bomb the missile sites. One member of the Joint Chiefs argued for using nuclear weapons immediately. Though that was not approved, a nuclear war was indeed very possible. Anytime the two superpowers stood toe to toe this way, there was a danger of thermonuclear war. Not a few Americans drew that conclusion. Fearing the worst, some left city homes for the "safety" of rural areas miles away.

In the midst of the crisis, the Cubans shot down a U-2 plane flying over their territory. Some members of the Ex Com felt this should be the signal for an invasion, but President Kennedy decided to wait. He suppressed the news lest it add fuel to the fires. Meantime letters were going back and forth between him and Khrushchev.

That fateful week the world waited with bated breath while Soviet ships moved toward American lines in the Caribbean. Finally, on Sunday, October 28, Khrushchev backed down. As Secretary of State Dean Rusk put it, the two superpowers were "eyeball to eyeball," and "somebody blinked." Khrushchev agreed to send the missiles back to the Soviet Union. In return, the United States made a secret pledge—confirmed years later by President Nixon—that the United States would not invade Cuba or permit any further hostile actions against it by Cuban exiles from Florida.

After it was over, Attorney General Robert Kennedy said that the world had been brought "to the abyss of nuclear destruction and the end of mankind." President Kennedy said that regardless of who would have pushed the button first—we or the Russians—the two nations would have suffered "150 million fatalities in the first eighteen hours," and more later. Everything that the United States had worked for in the previous three hundred years would have been destroyed in those eighteen hours. "Even the fruits of victory," Kennedy stated, "would be ashes in our mouths."

There were two other close calls in the thousand days Kennedy was President, but they were not nearly so frightening as the October Missile Crisis. In fact, they were not generally known until after Kennedy was assassinated. The first one had to do with Laos, a small country once ruled by France—and part of Indochina—where a civil war was raging. President

Kennedy decided during the first weeks of his administration to pressure the Communists—who were winning—to cease hostilities and join a three-sided government (rightists, "neutralists," and Communists). He let the word filter out to Moscow that if the Pathet Lao (the Communist group) refused to stop fighting, the United States would send its own troops into that country.

According to Kennedy's chief aide, Theodore Sorenson, the President wanted to avoid military action. But in the meantime the Pathet Lao were making impressive inroads. At a meeting of the National Security Council on May 1, 1961, the majority favored landing troops in Laos, as well as in Thailand and South Vietnam.

If the Pathet Lao still did not agree to a cease-fire, the recommendation was for an air attack coupled with "tactical nuclear weapons." If North Vietnamese or Chinese then moved in, Sorenson reports, the suggestion was that "their homelands would be bombed. If massive Red troops were then mobilized, nuclear bombs would be threatened and, if necessary, carried out. If the Soviets intervened, we should be prepared to accept the possibility of a general war."

Remembering the foiled Bay of Pigs invasion, Kennedy was careful. He took one step at a time. First, naval forces, two air squadrons, and 5000 marines were sent to Thailand. Then British, Australian and New Zealander units also were dispatched to the area, and diplomatic pressure was put on the Soviet Union to secure the cease-fire. But while this was going on, the Pathet Lao decided to accept the United States offer.

The second "small" nuclear crisis in Kennedy's day centered on West Berlin. Before the war there had been only one Berlin and one Germany. It had been the hope of the allies, including the Soviet Union, that Germany would remain a single nation. But differences between the United States, Britain, and France on the one side, and the Soviet Union on the other, ultimately led to two Germanys and two Berlins. West Berlin—associated with West Germany—was actually a hundred miles inside the territory of Communist-controlled German Democratic Republic (East Germany). To get there, you had to drive either on East German roads or fly over East German air space. Threats were always being made to cut off that access.

At a meeting between Khrushchev and Kennedy in Vienna, in June 1961, the Soviet leader announced he would sign a peace treaty with East Germany and turn over to it the matter of the "Berlin corridor." He had made the same threat during the Eisenhower administration, raising the possibility that the East Germans would deny access to West Berlin—and slowly choke it to death.

Upon his return from Vienna, Kennedy was given a plan prepared by the Joint Chiefs of Staff. If access to West Berlin were cut off, the plan called for small military actions along the autobahn (turnpike) to Berlin. And if that didn't work, the military would start dropping nuclear bombs. Many of his civilian counselors advised Kennedy to declare a "national emergency" immediately, triple the number of young men drafted into the Army, call up million reserve troops, bring home the wives and children of diplomats in Europe, and increase the military budget by a few billion dollars.

Kennedy felt that it would be better to move more slowly, but he and everyone else in high places agreed that in the end the United States might have to resort to nuclear war. The only difference between the national security members was whether to order one big nuclear assault against the Soviet Union or to engage in "careful and discriminate attack." No one was giving up the option of atomic weapons; the difference was simply over timing and intensity.

The December deadline came and went; nothing happened.

The Soviets did not carry out their threat. The crisis subsided. All that was left to show for it was the wall of bricks that East Germany had built between East and West Berlin. That Berlin Wall was meant to prevent East German citizens from fleeing to the West—either to reunite with their families or to live in a freer climate. But nothing more occurred. No war broke out. The nuclear threat was left hanging. It was very lucky for the human race.

7. MUTUAL ASSURED DESTRUCTION

"NO ONE CAN WIN A MODERN WAR. EVEN THE VICTOR LOSES."
General Curtis E. LeMay

In physics, we say that "every action has a reaction." In a speech on September 18, 1967, Secretary of Defense McNamara expressed regret that this was also happening with the nuclear-arms race. Whatever the intentions of either side may be, he said, if one side builds up its forces, the other side follows suit. It is "this action-reaction phenomenon," he declared, "that fuels an arms race."

The United States, according to McNamara, wanted to avoid such competition by reaching an understanding with the Soviet Union. Other American leaders made the same point. Assistant Secretary of Defense John McNaughton said in 1962 that we must "concern ourselves with the factors of stability. . . ." So did President Kennedy on a number of occasions.

The word heard with increasing frequency during the 1960's was "deterrence." As McNamara defined it, American policy was "to deter a deliberate nuclear attack . . . by maintaining a clear and convincing capability to inflict unacceptable damage on an attacker." In other words, if the Soviet Union knew that it would suffer "unacceptable damage" even if it struck first, it would not attack. The same was true of the United States: if it knew it would be badly hurt by Soviet retaliation, it wouldn't strike first. Supposedly, this "balance of terror"—stalemate—made both superpowers safe. It made them hesitant about pushing the button.

Of course there was always the danger that war might break out by accident or because of miscalculation. There are five known occasions, for instance, when the misreading of radar almost led to nuclear war. The first one was the "flock of geese" incident already related. There were at least four others. In addition, there were minor misreadings every few days. A congressional study showed that in a eighteen-month period during 1979 and 1980, there were 151 false alerts, lasting from a few seconds to six minutes. For example, a radar station at Mount Hebo, Oregon, mistook a piece of space debris reentering the atmosphere for a submarine-launched Soviet missile, and predicted it would strike the United States. The Pentagon claims that such alarms are routine and always caught in time.

In addition there were accidents, known as "broken arrows." According to the Defense Department, there have been twenty-seven major and seventy minor accidents involving nuclear weapons between 1950 and 1980—and there may have been several more. One occurred in 1961, after two nuclear bombs were dropped over Goldsboro, North Carolina, when the B-52 bomber carrying them crashed. The larger one, a 24-megaton weapon, almost 2,000 times as powerful as the Hiroshima bomb, had six safety switches. Five of them were tripped when the parachute cords attached to the bomb were caught in a tree and jolted the device. One switch held —and prevented what could have been one of the worst catastrophes in all history.

Another accident occurred over Palomares, Spain, on January 17, 1966, when a B-52 and a KC-135 refueling tanker collided, resulting in five deaths and the jettisoning of four H-bombs. One landed in a dry riverbed; two fell into a populated area where they released radioactivity; the fourth dropped into the ocean, and it took almost three months to find it.

Apart from the immediate damage caused by a "broken arrow," there is always the possibility that the United States or the U.S.S.R. will mistake one of these accidents for a real nuclear attack—and retaliate. War by accident or miscalculation, therefore, has always been a grave concern for the strategists.

Leaving accidents aside, however, McNamara speculated that the nuclear race could be stabilized. Both sides now knew that in the missile age there was no *physical* defense. There was only a *psychological* defense. The two superpowers were deterred from attacking each other because they were aware that regardless of who struck first, both would be devastated.

"The blunt, inescapable fact remains that the Soviet Union could still effectively destroy the United States," McNamara wrote, "even after absorbing the full weight of an American first strike." And that was equally true the other way around: the United States could destroy the Soviet Union, even after a surprise Soviet attack.

McNamara coined a new term for what the United States needed to guarantee security—"mutual assured destruction," or MAD. The United States would have an effective deterrent, said McNamara, if it always had the ability to kill 20 to 25 percent of the Soviet people and destroy half its industrial facilities. If it could absorb the first blow and still wreak that much damage on the Soviet Union, it was safe from attack. The United States, of course, was already far beyond that point of "mutual assured destruction."

General Maxwell Taylor told President Kennedy that 100 to

200 missiles were enough for "deterrence." That was a figure used by other people in the White House in the early 1960's. During the later part of the decade, the United States had more than 2,200 delivery vehicles—land-based missiles, submarine-launched missiles, and bombers. According to McNamara, more than half this force would survive *any* Soviet attack. And the United States would still be able—after such a blow—to kill two out of every five Russians.

Presumably the nuclear race could be stabilized at this point.

American leaders, however, insisted on being able to meet every challenge, no matter how remote. They were not satisfied with MAD. Early in the decade, intelligence agencies had reported that the Soviets were building an antiballistic missile (ABM) system around Moscow. Conceivably, Soviet ABMs might soon be able to shoot down incoming United States missiles, thus significantly reducing America's offensive power.

As it turned out, the ABM had too many flaws to be effective. It was vulnerable to decoys and electronic jamming, and it couldn't be made efficient enough to prevent *some* ICBMs and SLBMs from coming through. According to Dr. Daniel Fink, a former deputy director of Defense Research and Engineering, the ordinary offensive missile was reliable 41 to 65 percent of the time. Defensive missiles—ABMs—would be even less trustworthy. An enemy only had to increase the *number* of offensive missiles to overwhelm the ABM system.

American scientists and think-tankers had been discussing an *anti*missile missile since 1954. If you could destroy the enemy's missiles in flight, they reasoned, you had an excellent formula for winning. The United States would be able to save almost all of its people and property, whereas the Soviet Union would be annihilated by the Pentagon's *offensive* missiles.

On paper the idea was attractive. But the plan had been vetoed by Eisenhower and rejected by Kennedy because—among other reasons—there was no radar system adequate to the task. Lyndon Johnson revived the hope of an ABM defense in 1967–68, when he coaxed $1.9 billion out of a suspicious Congress. And President Richard Nixon went further; he asked for an initial expenditure of $7.2 billion.

The Safeguard (ABM) system was exciting to contemplate. It called for two kinds of radar to track down enemy missiles in the last ten minutes of their flight. Once the radar "found" the incoming weapon, it would be "killed" by either a Spartan or a Sprint. X rays from the Spartan (which had a range of a few hundred miles) would intercept and destroy in the stratosphere. Neutrons from the Sprint would intercept and destroy in the atmosphere. The original plan was to establish twelve sites for the Safeguard system in the continental United States and one each in Hawaii and Alaska.

It was an elaborate idea, but even Nixon was forced to concede that an effective ABM was "not now within our power." Under President Ford, the only ABM site in the country—at Grand Forks, North Dakota—was allowed to stand inactive.

As for the Russians, they too talked about producing ABMs capable of "destroying missiles in flight." But they were never able to make the kind of antimissile missile that could really do it.

Despite the general belief that the ABM was of little value, strategists in Washington decided to produce a counter-weapon to it. Engineers and scientists designed the MIRV—multiple independently targeted reentry vehicle—for that purpose. By putting a *cluster* of warheads on each United States missile, the enemy's ABM system would be exhausted. It might shoot down the first warhead, but the second, third, and fourth would get through.

This was the original idea behind development of the MIRV —as a counterweapon to Soviet ABMs. But as it became evident that Soviet ABMs were little danger, the Pentagon found an entirely different purpose for the MIRV—one that gave the United States a big edge and caused the Soviet Union to try and catch up. Instead of stability, therefore, there was instability. An American action caused a Soviet reaction.

In its new role the MIRV was modified so that its cluster of reentry vehicles (each with a warhead) would hit separate targets. Instead of being a defense against the ABM, it would be an offensive weapon against Soviet cities and silos. A single "space bus" would expel reentry vehicles at different trajectories, making it possible for each one to hit a different target. One would head toward Moscow, another toward Leningrad, a third toward Minsk. Instead of one missile aimed at one city or silo, it would now be aimed at three to fourteen. The MIRV was authorized in 1964. Within two years the Johnson administration was given authorization to replace the old Minuteman I, which had one warhead, with the Minuteman III, carrying three warheads. On thirty-one submarines, the Polaris missile, carrying one to three warheads was to be replaced by the Poseidon, carrying ten to fourteen.

The Soviet Union, of course, responded in kind. Moscow didn't test its own MIRV until 1973, but in the meantime it increased its supply of single-warhead ICBMs from 200 in late 1964 to 340 in 1966, 730 in 1967, and 1,600 by 1972. Ultimately it caught up with, and even surpassed, the United States in the number of missiles. But since its missiles carried only one warhead apiece, the Soviets remained behind the United States in the number of *warheads.* That, too, the Russians tried to correct.

The Soviets began work on more advanced missiles. One of them, the SS-18, was built to carry thirty reentry vehicles and warheads—far more than any comparable United States missile, even the MX. As for nuclear submarines, the Soviets increased the number to 62 (as against 41 for the United States). And although those 62 still carry single-warhead missiles, the Delta class of Soviet submarines, some of which are already operational, carry MIRV missiles—missiles with many warheads.

Again, an action by the United States sparked a reaction by the Soviet Union. Neither side was better off than previously.

Not long before he left office, Secretary of Defense McNamara presented new figures on what might happen in a nuclear exchange. He computed the results under three "postures," or circumstances: (1) where the United States did nothing to improve defense, (2) where it spent $9.9 billion for antimissile devices to protect twenty-five cities, and (3) where it spent $19.9 billion to protect fifty cities.

The computer printout was disheartening. If the Soviets struck first and the United States retaliated, the results were the same in all three postures: 120 million American dead, more than 120 million Soviet dead. The expenditure on defense would be for nothing. If the United States struck first and the Soviets retaliated, there would be 100 million American dead under the first posture, 90 million under the other two. The number of Russian dead in each instance, however, would be 70 million. The reason the Russians would lose fewer people is that many United States weapons would be used against Soviet missile silos, leaving fewer to destroy their cities. In all cases, both societies would lose three quarters of their industrial facilities.

It would be wrong to say that no efforts were made to ease tensions between the two superpowers. A number of treaties were signed during the 1960's placing limits on aspects of the arms race. But most were of a minor nature, and the others had serious weaknesses. The arms race hardly paused for breath.

In December 1959 twelve nations, including the United States and the Soviet Union, signed a treaty prohibiting military activity or testing in the Antarctic–South Pole area. On September 20, 1961, the two superpowers agreed to a set of principles for disarmament negotiations. It was an excellent document, calling for "disbanding of armed forces . . . elimination of all stockpiles of nuclear, chemical, bacteriological, and other weapons of mass destruction . . . elimination of all means of delivery of weapons of mass destruction . . . cessation of military training . . . discontinuance of military expenditures." But no treaty was ever negotiated embodying these principles. The McCloy-Zorin document, as it was named after its two negotiators, remained a dead letter.

In June 1963 Kennedy and Khrushchev approved a "hot-line" agreement for direct communication between the leaders of the two countries. Should an emergency occur—say, as a result of an accidental discharge of a nuclear weapon—the leaders would be able immediately to speak with each other to contain the crisis. Less than two months later the test ban treaty was signed in Moscow, but this, as already noted was flawed by the fact that it permitted testing underground.

For the next thirteen years talks between the great powers continued, agreements were signed, but the results were meager. No one gave up anything important. Not a single nuclear weapon was destroyed; indeed the level of armaments continued to spiral upward. Pacts were concluded, for instance, to prohibit nuclear weapons in outer space, in Latin America, on the seabeds. The United States and the Soviet Union agreed to consult each other if there was an accidental explosion. But none of this was of great significance.

Two understandings *were* important. One was the Non-Proliferation Treaty (NPT). Signed in 1968, it was later ratified by over a hundred nations. As the name suggests, it was an agreement not to increase the number of countries having nuclear arms. Under its terms, the five nations that had nuclear stockpiles in 1968—the United States, the U.S.S.R., Britain, France, and China—were expected not to give or sell nuclear weapons to other countries. The non-nuclear countries were expected not to buy or make any on their own. In return the "have" nations pledged to "pursue negotiations in good faith" for "cessation of the nuclear arms race at an early date."

There were many problems with NPT. To begin with, two of the five nuclear nations—China and France—refused to sign it. Another country that would soon test a nuclear bomb—India—also held out, as did West Germany, Japan, Israel, South Africa, Italy, Libya, and others. There were also a number of loopholes in the treaty—for instance, that signers could conduct nuclear explosions for "peaceful" purposes, such as leveling a mountain or digging a canal. And enforcement of the agreement was loose and ineffective.

A second treaty that could have—but didn't—change world history was SALT I. SALT—Strategic Arms Limitation Talks—had its origins in 1964. With prospects for general disarmament poor, it occurred to some delegates at the United Nations that something more limited might have a chance of approval. Instead of full-scale disarmament, they urged as a first step a freeze on strategic nuclear weapons. Each side would agree not to produce or deploy any more than they had at that time.

When Lyndon Johnson approved the idea it seemed it would sail through with ease. But there were soon complications. Johnson added the word "verified" to "freeze." He wanted a sizable number of international inspectors on Soviet territory to see to it that Moscow lived up to a freeze agreement. This, of course, rankled the Russians. The Soviets, for their part, refused to consider a freeze unless it was coupled with a reduction—in other words, they wanted both to freeze and reduce the number of nuclear weapons.

There the matter stood for a number of years—until 1968, when Johnson and Soviet Premier Alexei Kosygin agreed to try their hand at "arms limitation." Again, however, there was a new obstacle. The Soviets sent armed forces into Czechoslovakia in August of that year to remove the government of Alexander Dubcek, which had proclaimed "socialism with a human face." President Johnson reacted by calling off arms talks. Finally, in November 1969, a year after Richard Nixon was elected, negotiators for both sides began talking in Helsinki, Finland.

It took another three years (and 434 bargaining sessions) before Henry Kissinger and Soviet Foreign Minister Andrei Gromyko finally came to terms. SALT I actually contained two agreements. One limited the two superpowers to two ABM sites and 100 ABM launchers at each site. Subsequently the parties agreed to cut back to one site each, and even that was dispensed with by President Ford.

The second pact, the Interim Agreement, as it was called, did not provide for either cutbacks or a freeze. Instead it set limits on nuclear *increases*. The United States would be permitted to expand the number of nuclear submarines from 41 to 44 (with 710 missiles). The Soviet Union was allowed to build up from its existing 30 to 62 (with 950 missiles).

On land, the United States was authorized to have 1,000 ICBMs; the Russians, 1,410. All of these numbers for land-based missiles were higher than what both sides had at the time. Furthermore, nothing was done to curb improvement in *quality*. Missing, for instance, was a curb on MIRVs—placing multiple warheads on each missile—or on making weapons more accurate. Doubling the accuracy of a warhead—say, from a half mile to a quarter of a mile—increases its "lethality"—kill capacity—by eight times. But SALT I had no provisions against such improvements.

In the end the idea of a freeze was forgotten, and SALT I became a means of escalation—by mutual agreement.

Another SALT treaty was negotiated with the Soviet Union by Presidents Gerald Ford and Jimmy Carter, but it followed the same pattern. Under its terms each side was allowed to increase the number of strategic warheads by about 4,000, as well as to improve weapon quality. Even so, the Senate refused to ratify it during Carter's term. A new President, Ronald Reagan, called its provisions unfair and suggested new negotiations.

From 1965 through 1972, the nuclear issue took second place in most American minds. First place was occupied by the biggest "little war" in American history, Vietnam. Nonetheless the nuclear issue did not subside.

The Vietnam war was rooted in ancient colonialism. The three segments of Indochina—Vietnam, Cambodia, and Laos —had been ruled by France for almost three quarters of a century. During World War II, Indochina was occupied by Japan, but a resistance movement was formed under the leadership of a Communist, Ho Chi Minh. The United States supported this resistance group, called the Viet Minh.

But when they were not granted full independence after the war, the Vietnamese turned against France. Now the United States did an about-face. It threw its support to the French, gave them billions of aid, and, when they were on the verge of defeat, offered them three nuclear weapons.

Despite that, however, France was defeated. Accords signed in Geneva, Switzerland, on July 20, 1954, divided the country temporarily in two parts—until elections could be held in 1956. The elections, however, were never held—probably because the man who had been installed in power at the behest of the United States, Ngo Dinh Diem, could not win. Instead there was a rigged referendum for president of South Vietnam alone in October 1955, which gave Diem 98.2 percent of the vote.

The United States contributed hundreds of millions of dollars to Diem and trained both his troops and police. In the next few years, repression grew by leaps and bounds. According to a French expert, as many as 75,000 people may have been killed in this campaign. In the face of this repression tribesmen and former Viet Minh fighters retreated to the forests for a new guerrilla war. In December 1960 they formed the National Liberation Front.

From then until Diem fell from power and was assassinated in 1963, the government lost ground steadily. It lost ground despite the fact that the United States had sent 22,000 military "advisers" to help Diem. The advisers, incidentally, did more than advise; they flew combat planes, some directed troops.

On August 2, 1964, two American destroyers were allegedly attacked by North Vietnamese PT boats in the Tonkin Gulf. The incident still is cloaked in controversy, with critics claiming that the destroyers were acting as cover for a South Vietnamese assault on North Vietnamese islands. Be that as it may, the incident stirred great passions in the United States. With almost no opposition in Congress, President Johnson was given authority to take measures "to prevent further aggression." It was this Tonkin Gulf resolution that the President used as legal justification for sending troops to fight in Vietnam.

This was the easiest war in American history to get into; the hardest one to end. The 23,000 American troops in South Vietnam in 1964 rose to 185,000 the next year, 385,000 in 1966, 485,000 in 1967, and a peak of 542,000 in 1968. From 1965 to early 1970, the United States dropped 4.5 million tons of TNT on Vietnam—considerably more than was dropped on Germany during World War II. In addition to the half million American troops, there were 65,000 from South Korea (paid for by the United States), and contingents from the Philippines, Australia, and New Zealand. The South Vietnamese government had nearly a million men in its armed services and auxiliaries.

But this massive force was unable to defeat a quarter of a million Vietcong (as the South Vietnamese guerrillas were called) and North Vietnamese. The Vietnamese suffered fearful losses—a million civilian casualties alone. But the United States also lost heavily—55,000 dead and 300,000 wounded.

Soon the largest antiwar movement in American history was attracting millions of citizens to its banner. On a number of occasions hundreds of thousands of people demonstrated against the war. At least two million people in scores of cities throughout the country held protest actions on October 15, 1969. Exactly a month later, 780,000 congregated in Washington for the largest antiwar rally in United States history. Young men burned their draft cards in public ceremonies, and here and there an act of violence broke out. With so much opposition at home, Nixon agreed to pull American troops out of Vietnam early in 1973.

The war between Communists and anti-Communist forces continued, however, until 1975, when South Vietnamese troops, under President Nguyen Van Thieu, simply fell apart. The Vietcong and North Vietnamese took the reins and unified the country under Communist leadership.

During this long and bitter conflict, all the fighting was done with conventional weapons—tanks, planes, rifles. But there were four occasions when the United States contemplated the use of nuclear bombs in Indochina. Two have already been related—the offer of atom bombs to France when it faced defeat in 1954, and the 1961 plan to use such weapons in Laos if Communist guerrillas did not stop fighting.

Seven years later, in 1968, the nuclear option was considered again. American marines were surrounded at their base in Khe Sanh. During the siege President Johnson queried the chairman of the Joint Chiefs of Staff as to whether he would have to use nuclear weapons to hold that base. Johnson said he wanted to avoid that kind of decision, if possible.

Nevertheless General William C. Westmoreland, commander of the American forces in Vietnam, formed "a small secret group" in Saigon to study a possible "nuclear defense of Khe Sanh." Westmoreland tells us this story in an autobiography, *War in Vain.* He reasoned, he says, that small nuclear bombs would send "a message" to Hanoi, just as the first two atom bombs in 1945 had sent a message to Japan.

The nuclear option for Vietnam was weighed even more seriously by Richard Nixon. When he was running for President in 1968, Nixon said he had a plan to end the war, but he couldn't reveal it because he did not want to jeopardize steps toward peace by President Johnson. In a book published eleven years later, H. R. Haldeman, Nixon's chief of staff, disclosed what that plan was. Nixon himself called it the Madman Theory.

The idea was to get word to North Vietnam that Nixon was a "madman" when it came to the question of communism. "I want the North Vietnamese to believe I've reached the point where I might do *anything* to stop the war," Nixon told Haldeman. "We'll just slip the word to them that 'for God's sake, you know Nixon is obsessed about communism. We can't restrain him when he's angry—and he has his hand on the nuclear button. . . .'" Nixon was confident this threat would bring Communist leader Ho Chi Minh to "Paris in two days, begging for peace." He set November 1969 as the deadline for the North Vietnamese to accept his terms or face the consequences —including a nuclear attack. The nuclear targets were picked out and a speech to the American people, announcing the escalation, was drafted.

Once again, however, the Vietnamese were spared the devastation of a nuclear attack. As Haldeman tells it, Kissinger "found the North Vietnamese absolutely intractable." They wouldn't even negotiate under this threat. The reason, according to Nixon's chief aide, was that "the American people had turned against the war. The young were saying they wouldn't fight it." The North Vietnamese were convinced therefore that it was only a matter of time before "the United States would have to pull out."

Nixon makes the same point in his own memoirs. "The only chance for an ultimatum to succeed," he writes, "was to convince the communists that I could depend on solid support at home." But there was no such support. Nixon had to back away from his nuclear threat lest it provoke ever greater protests.

8. A LITTLE BIG WAR

President Nixon, like President Johnson, was preoccupied with the war in Vietnam. He had hoped to be through with it by November 1969, but the war went on and on, throughout his whole first term in office. Understandably, then, Nixon's nuclear strategy was a replay of Johnson's and Kennedy's. What his Defense Secretary, Melvin R. Laird, called a "spectrum of conflict" was approximately what McNamara had called a "graduated" or "flexible" response. The United States must be prepared, said Laird, to fight an all-out nuclear war, a nuclear war in Europe, a conventional war in Europe, and a local war somewhere else. It must be prepared, in other words, for anything, though at the moment the focus was on the "nasty" little war in Southeast Asia.

Nonetheless Nixon considered using nuclear weapons at least twice during his six years in office. (He resigned in August 1974, two years early, because of the Watergate scandal.) The first, as described in the last chapter, was at the beginning of his administration, when he threatened to use the bomb unless

North Vietnam and the Vietcong came to terms. The second involved the Soviet Union more directly.

On October 6, 1973—the Jewish Day of Atonement, Yom Kippur—100,000 Egyptian soldiers crossed into the Israeli-held Sinai Peninsula. For the next two and a half weeks the fighting between Israel on the one hand and Egypt and Syria on the other was indecisive. The Israelis were unable to defeat their Arab adversaries with the same speed—six days—as in the previous Middle East war in 1967. Considering Israel's small population, its casualties were alarming.

After a couple of weeks the United States and the Soviet Union arranged for a cease-fire. The relationship between the superpowers at the moment had improved. The previous year, the twelve basic principles of *detente* (an easing of tension) had been formulated at a Moscow summit meeting between Nixon and Brezhnev, and the two leaders had approved the first SALT agreement. They were both anxious to avoid a wider conflict in the Middle East.

But the Israelis were slow to put the cease-fire into effect. They had surrounded 100,000 Egyptian troops in the Sinai, and they felt that within a few days they could *win* the war—instead of allowing it to end in a stalemate. That did not sit well with the Soviets. On October 24, Brezhnev told Nixon on the hot line: "If the Israelis are not going to adhere to the cease-fire, let us [both] work together to impose a cease-fire, if necessary by force."

The United States rejected this suggestion. Thereupon the Soviet Union sent a ship loaded with nuclear weapons to Alexandria, Egypt. Egypt already had Soviet-made "Scud" missiles, capable of delivering nuclear bombs. Brezhnev further hinted that if the cease-fire was not observed by Israel, the Soviets might send troops to enforce it. That would place Russian forces in the Middle East for the first time, something the

United States could be expected to oppose vigorously.

For fifteen hours the world faced another crisis like the one eleven years earlier—the Cuban Missile Crisis. Few people knew what was happening, because neither Nixon nor Brezhnev advised the public that a nuclear confrontation might be in the making.

But at 11 P.M. that night, Secretary of State Henry Kissinger called together high officials for an emergency meeting at the White House. After a brief discussion the United States declared a worldwide DefCon 3 alert. ("DefCon" means Defense Condition. Defense Condition 5 is the normal state of peace, DefCon 1 is war, DefCon 3 is somewhere in the middle.) An aircraft carrier was dispatched at full speed to the Mediterranean. The Strategic Air Command, which has charge over B-52 bombers and missiles, was placed on an advance alert. And the Sixth Fleet, patrolling the Mediterranean Sea, was put on DefCon 2—just one stage away from a nuclear war.

Speaking to the press next morning, October 25, Kissinger warned the Russians not to "transplant the great power rivalry into the Middle East." He advised them, instead, to fulfill their "special duty to see to it that confrontations are kept within bounds that do not threaten civilized life."

Fortunately, before things could get further out of hand, Israel halted its offensive. The Soviets withdrew their ship. The crisis ended.

The near confrontation of 1973 showed how fragile was the nuclear stalemate. The policy of deterrence did not always deter, and the agreement signed in 1972 for detente didn't entirely ease tensions. Each side continued producing new wonder weapons and devising new strategies.

When James Schlesinger was appointed Defense Secretary by Nixon in 1973, he inherited a technological harvest. On the drawing boards or in production were such weapons as the MIRV, the MARV (maneuverable reentry vehicle), the Trident submarine and Trident missile, the cruise missile, the B-1 bomber.

The emphasis in the 1940's had been on the fission (atom) bomb; in the 1950's on the fusion (hydrogen) bomb; in the 1960's on the ballistic missile and nuclear submarine. Now, in the 1970's, the focus shifted to making weapons more accurate. Accuracy is important because it greatly increases the "lethality" of a warhead. A 100-kiloton warhead that comes within 300 yards of its target will be eight times as destructive as a 100-kiloton bomb that explodes 600 yards from the target. Double the accuracy, in other words, and you increase the "kill" capability immensely.

An important element of the new weaponry was the MIRV —the multiple independently targeted reentry vehicle—which allows a single missile to carry two, three, five, ten, or more reentry vehicles (RVs). The reentry vehicle is a special capsule that carries the bomb.

Ordinarily the missile carrying these RVs goes through three stages. In the first one it is propelled through the atmosphere by rocket motors. Then it coasts through the stratosphere— stage two. Finally it re-enters the atmosphere thousands of miles away, headed toward its target at the speed of a bullet (that is why it is called a *ballistic* missile; *bullet* is derived from the French word for "ball"). The missile is preprogrammed; that means its trajectory and velocity are determined in advance.

The MIRV adds new features to the missile. To begin with, there are several reentry vehicles on each one. These are attached to the front of the missile, called the *bus*, and covered with a nose cone. After the rocket motors fall off, the cone is also ejected; the bus coasts along in space, dropping its RVs at predetermined targets. By arranging for the bus to move sideways, each reentry vehicle can be launched at a different target. This was a major breakthrough, for in this way many more silos or cities can be destroyed with the same number of missiles.

The next step on the engineering agenda was to make reentry vehicles more accurate. They don't have to be too accurate to wreck a city; even if they land a mile or two from the center of town, they will make a shambles of it. The Hiroshima bomb in 1945 destroyed brick buildings and severely damaged steel construction 1.2 miles from where it exploded (ground zero). But a 20-megaton bomb today—both superpowers have them in abundance—would cause similar wreckage 10.5 miles away in all directions, as well as first-degree burns 27 miles away, and radiation damage still much farther away. Little would be left of a major city like Chicago.

A missile silo, however, is surrounded by so much concrete that an attacking missile must come fairly close to knock it out of commission. Secretary McNamara estimated in the 1960's that six missiles would have to be launched against each enemy silo. Engineers and scientists began working on lowering this ratio, and in due course developed the maneuverable reentry vehicle (MARV).

In the early days, if a missile was off course, it could only be corrected during the first stage of its flight—when the rocket motors were still burning. It couldn't be corrected in the last two—as it coasted through space and as it reentered the atmosphere toward its target. But with the MIRV, improved navigation, and now the MARV, scientists and engineers found a way to maneuver the reentry vehicle in the last stages of flight.

They developed the global positioning system (GPS), which allows the missile computer to determine where the missile is, and exactly how fast it is going. And they added weights, flaps, and sensors to the reentry vehicle. The result is an RV that can be guided toward its objective even as it decends into the atmosphere again. It has "eyes" to see the target as it comes close; it then compares what it "sees" with a map in its computer. Finally it maneuvers itself toward the object it is supposed to hit. It can even change direction, if necessary, to evade defensive missiles.

Another accuracy weapon developed in the 1970's was the cruise missile. This is a delivery vehicle, 14 to 20 feet long and only 21 inches in diameter. It is supported by small wings and propelled by jet engines. Capable of being launched from a plane, a submarine, a surface vessel, or a missile launcher on land, the cruise flies at treetop level to avoid enemy radar. It also has a computer that matches what it "sees" with a map and can zero in on a target 2,000 miles away within 100 feet. An added advantage is that it is very cheap—only $1.4 million per missile.

The missile experimental (MX) is the latest and perhaps most sensational of the accuracy weapons. With 10 MARVs on each one, the MX will have twice the explosive power and three times the accuracy of Minuteman III missiles. It will be able to hit a target 8,000 miles away within 35 yards. Moreover, unlike the Titan or Minuteman, the MX will be *mobile.* It is hoped the Russians will never know exactly where an MX—constantly in motion and hidden—is at a given time and will therefore not be able to aim at it accurately.

The accuracy of a weapon is listed as CEP ("circular error probable"). If a missile has a CEP of a quarter of a mile, it means that 50 percent of those missiles will land within a quarter of a mile and 50 percent will land outside that circle. In the earlier part of the 1970's, Soviet missiles had a CEP of two thirds of a mile. A few years later newer Soviet ICBMs had a CEP of a quarter to three tenths of a mile. The SS-18, for instance, has a CEP of 1,500 feet.

American missiles were at approximately these levels of accuracy to begin with in the 1970's. A Minuteman II missile, for instance, had a CEP of three tenths of a mile. But the accuracy improvements introduced in that decade changed this drastically. The reentry vehicle of a Trident 2 missile is expected to have a CEP of 90 to 300 feet. The same is true of the MX. According to present calculations, a Soviet SS-18 missile (the most accurate one in their arsenal) has a 27 percent chance of killing a hard missile silo. The Minuteman III, by contrast, has a 55 percent chance, and an MX (when it is deployed) will have an 80 percent chance. So will the Trident 2 missile.

As was to be expected, the accuracy weapons caused an important modification of nuclear strategy. James R. Schlesinger, once a professor at the University of Virginia, was appointed Secretary of Defense in May 1973, just a few months after the United States agreed to get out of Vietnam. The image of America as an invincible power was badly battered. And the McNamara strategy of graduated response was tarnished.

Schlesinger drafted a new nuclear strategy to fit the circumstances—a strategy he felt would boost American self-confidence. With the MIRVs, MARVs, Tridents, cruise missiles, and others awaiting production and deployment, he composed a nuclear policy to take advantage of their unique characteristic —accuracy. He called it "restrained counterforce."

It was not realistic, Schlesinger said, to talk about destroying the Soviet Union's cities in one big attack, because the Soviet Union would destroy our cities in return. We and they both had large numbers of missiles on "invulnerable" submarines— vehicles safe from attack because they could not be tracked down by any present devices. Those invulnerable submarines (as well as some bombers) could destroy the other side's cities regardless of who struck first.

The realistic thing, therefore, was to plan for a *limited*—not a total—war, and to forget about "killing" the cities. The main focus of America's nuclear weapons should be Russia's missile silos, military airfields, and command posts.

In a book he had written years before, the Secretary suggested that "we must become adjusted to the heavy costs of limited warfare as a condition of life. . . ." Schlesinger designed such a program. It called for "selective response options— smaller and more precisely focused than in the past."

That would require, on the one hand, beefing up conventional forces to fight "small," *automated* wars. Instead of depending on human power, as in Vietnam, the United States would rely on remotely piloted drones, unmanned aircraft, and laser-guided weapons. The drones—without pilots and directed from far behind the lines—would photograph the enemy haunts. Based on this information, unmanned aircraft would fly to the targets and release highly accurate laser-guided conventional weapons.

The second, and main, feature of the Schlesinger Doctrine was limited *nuclear* war. It proposed to make nuclear wars smaller—and therefore "fightable." A President might hesitate before ordering an all-out nuclear attack, said Schlesinger. But "small" nuclear weapons might not be so repugnant. They would "wound rather than kill."

The President, for instance, might give an Army colonel authority to set off nuclear mines to stop Soviet troops marching toward West Germany; or he might radio a submarine skipper to launch a missile at a Soviet military airfield. Each side, under this doctrine, would restrain itself and would avoid hitting cities.

It was a means, said Schlesinger, of sending them a message. Instead of a maximum attack the United States would initiate a minimum attack, then wait for the other side to respond—either with a minimum attack of its own or a plea for negotiations. If the enemy continued fighting, the United States would escalate in tandem—but refrain from all-out confrontation.

Schlesinger argued that if the Russians were willing to play this game, we might not get ourselves into such quagmires as Vietnam. We would threaten a limited nuclear war in the expectation the Soviets might back off. We would be less hesitant about making such a threat because leaders who would flinch from all-out nuclear wars that would destroy civilization wouldn't flinch, the Secretary said, from a limited war. The threat of a *controlled* war, therefore, was "believable."

How costly would a "restrained counterforce" war be? Secretary Schlesinger made an estimate for a Senate Foreign Relations subcommittee in September 1974. If the Soviet Union dispatched a single one-megaton bomb to each American ICBM field, "the number of fatalities [would be] up to about 800,000." Another million and a half would "fall ill as a result of radiation sickness coming from fallout," but would recover in due time.

The Senate subcommittee appointed a panel to review these figures. It was chaired by the President of the Massachusetts Institute of Technology, Jerome Weisner, and included many experts who had once worked for the Pentagon. The panel concluded that Schlesinger's figures were quite "unrealistic." The number of dead, its report said, would probably be "in the range of 3.5 to 22 million." In addition, there would be 800,-000 dead and 400,000 injured in *Canada.*

Many people disagreed with the Schlesinger Doctrine. In particular they disagreed that when the bombs started falling, American and Soviet leaders could restrain themselves. Senator Stuart Symington, who had once been an Air Force Secretary, told Schlesinger: "You talk as if the Joint Chiefs of Staff of the Soviet Union and the Joint Chiefs of Staff of the United States were together in this thing and started to play a game of chess." Limited nuclear wars were likely to get out of hand —a point President Kennedy had made years before. In his book *The Strategy of Peace,* Kennedy had written that "inevitably the use of small nuclear armaments will lead to larger nuclear armaments on both sides, until the worldwide holocaust has begun."

Despite the opposition, however, "restrained counterforce" became official United States policy. American leaders were "thinking the unthinkable"—nuclear war. General William Westmoreland stated that "the use of several small yield nuclear weapons conceivably could have put an end" to the Vietnam War.

A military officer in Seoul, Korea, told a press conference that the United States would now consider nuclear options "seriously." In June 1975 a report was leaked to the press that Strategic Air Command crews were being given "limited nuclear war training." Air Force bomber crews were asked to take a crash course in carrying out twenty-five different types of limited nuclear missions.

Moreover, the arsenal of tactical atomic arms was so extravagant that it was difficult to assume they were not for ready use. The United States had 8,500 strategic weapons at the time— warheads that could hit the Soviet Union from the United States. But it also had 22,000 tactical weapons, widely dispersed over the globe.

In Europe 2,250 aircraft, missile launchers, and nuclear cannon were equipped to deliver 7,000 warheads. (The Soviet stockpile of tactical nuclear warheads in Europe was between 3,000 and 3,500.) They were emplaced in every NATO country except Luxembourg, Norway, Denmark, and France—which had its own supply. In addition to air-to-surface bombs they included nuclear artillery shells, depth bombs, and atomic demolition munitions. For delivery, the Pentagon had a choice of 500 fighter-bombers and at least four kinds of surface-to-surface missiles—Lance, Sergeant, Honest John, and Pershing. There were also 1,700 tactical warheads in Asia, 1,500 aboard ships of the Pacific Fleet, and 10,000 at home.

One "small" bomb the Pentagon was developing for combat warfare stirred deep controversy—the enhanced-radiation bomb or, as it is known popularly, the neutron bomb. This is a small fission-fusion bomb ranging from less than one kiloton (equivalent to a thousand tons of TNT) to two kilotons.

In the scale of nuclear weapons, the neutron bomb is a midget—8 to 15 percent as powerful as the Hiroshima bomb. But its yield of radiation is six to ten times as high as that of the ordinary fission bomb. A one-kiloton neutron bomb has special shielding that limits destruction by blast and fire to 300 feet from the explosion. But the neutrons released have a more severe effect, killing and injuring people up to a mile away.

Those in the affected area are incapacitated within five minutes, suffering nausea, convulsions, and diarrhea from the neutron radiation. If the dose is heavy, some die within hours, others linger for 60 to 90 days, until they are overcome by delirium, respiratory failure, and coma.

Thus if Soviet tanks were moving toward American lines, the neutron bomb would put out of action the soldiers in those tanks, but leave the tanks themselves intact. Hence the neutron bomb became known as the weapon that killed people but saved property.

The neutron bomb was a subject of dispute, both in the United States and Europe, during all of the Carter administration. The decision as to whether or not to produce the weapon was delayed on a number of occasions. But in the first year of his administration, President Ronald Reagan ordered the Pentagon to start production of the 200-pound warhead. "This weapon was particularly designed," Reagan said, "to offset the great superiority that the Soviet Union has on the Western front against the NATO nations—a tank advantage of better than four to one."

The neutron bomb, in other words, was envisioned as a weapon to be used in a conventional war—against tanks, for instance. Critics, like Fred M. Kaplan, formerly at the Massachussetts Institute of Technology Center for International Studies, argue however that the neutron bomb is liable to provoke the all-out nuclear war it was intended to prevent. If the Russians faced the prospect of either surrendering or escalating the war to a full-scale nuclear exchange, Kaplan believes they would take the second alternative.

One risk of developing mininukes, warned Barry Schneider of the Center for Defense Information, "is that they may create the illusion that a limited war can be fought. . . . As smaller, 'cleaner,' and more accurate tactical nuclear weapons are added to the U.S. arsenal, they will add to the dangerous illusion that tactical nuclear weapons can be used with no risk of escalation."

A first cousin to the Schlesinger Doctrine of restrained counterforce was elaborated by the Carter administration a half dozen years later. In August 1980 President Jimmy Carter issued Presidential Directive 59 (PD-59) approving a strategy for "limited" nuclear war with the Soviet Union. As advertised by its supporters, this was conceived as a major step forward; it avoided the big, all-out war everyone feared would mean the end of both superpowers.

The "countervailing strategy"—elaborated primarily by Defense Secretary Harold Brown—foresaw a nuclear war against the Soviet Union that would last for weeks, even months. It would last that long, instead of a few hours, because the United States planned it that way. In Brown's scenario the United States would aim only at Soviet missile silos, command posts, airplane bases, and the like—counter*force*. It would spare cities and it would keep the attack geared to "appropriate levels of response." The Russians therefore would have an "incentive" to negotiate a settlement, lest they be met with the next higher level of response.

Brown called this a "continuum of options, ranging from use of small numbers of . . . weapons aimed at narrowly defined targets, to employment of large portions of our nuclear forces against a broad spectrum of targets." In other words, the attack would begin with a few warheads. The Russians, knowing that Washington was prepared to step up the attack (continuum of options), might then ask for peace. If it didn't, the attack weapons would become more numerous and the targets more important. At each stage, as Brown saw it, Moscow would have an incentive to quit—lest something worse happened. And the United States would be in a strong position for the next round because it would retain a "secure strategic reserve" —hidden or mobile weapons that Moscow could not get at, such as missiles on submarines.

Many years ago Herman Kahn wrote a book called *On Escalation*. It spelled out forty-four "rungs" of nuclear escalation, ending with such interesting ones as "slow-motion counter-'property' war," "countervalue salvo," "augmented disarming attack," and finally the "spasm of insensate war" —in which someone pushed the button in an "automatic, unthinking, and uncontrolled" fashion.

Presidential Directive 59, as expounded by Secretary Brown, was not stated as colorfully, but it has much the same reasoning behind it—namely, that the two sides would keep cool while large areas were being destroyed and millions of people torn apart or burned to death.

Brown admitted that limited nuclear strikes would have a strong possibility of escalating into all-out nuclear war. But he argued that we must not resign "ourselves to the inevitability of such escalation."

In his testimony to Congress, Brown indicated how terrifying a nuclear exchange would be. If a one-megaton bomb detonated on a major city, he said, it would kill just about everybody in a radius of 1.7 miles in all directions, and about half the people within 2.7 miles of ground zero. All told, there would be a quarter of a million immediate deaths.

In the limited attack on the United States ICBM force—the kind of war conceived by Presidential Directive 59—there would be "anywhere from 2 million to 22 million fatalities within thirty days," depending on wind, weather, and the height of burst.

With all that, Brown felt that "the controlled use of nuclear weapons . . . should enable us to provide leverage for a negotiated termination of the fighting."

The big question, as with Schlesinger's restrained-counterforce strategy, was whether the Soviets would play this game. Would the Soviets remain restrained as millions of their citizens perished and billions in property were destroyed? Would the American government remain restrained in a similar situation?

It was asking a lot of human nature to be so forbearing.

9. THE SECOND NUCLEAR AGE

"ONCE YOU START USING THESE WEAPONS
YOU ARE LIKELY TO GET INTO AN ALL-OUT WAR."
President Jimmy Carter

On May 18, 1974, to everyone's surprise, India exploded a 12-kiloton nuclear device, approximately the equivalent of the Hiroshima bomb, underground. It thus became the sixth member of the "nuclear club," behind the United States, the Soviet Union, Britain, France, and China.

What surprised—and angered—American leaders was the fuel India had used. It was plutonium—just as in many A-bombs or in the atomic triggers for hydrogen bombs. But it was plutonium reprocessed from the waste of three nuclear power reactors and from three research reactors. The other five members of the nuclear club had been making their nuclear bombs from either uranium-235 enriched in complex enrichment plants, or from plutonium-239 made in special reactors.

Both were intricate and expensive techniques that not many countries could afford. But reprocessing the waste of nuclear power reactors was another matter. It indicated that dozens of nations would soon be able to make nuclear bombs—and that was what worried the United States.

Atomic plants that generate electricity are usually fueled by small ceramic pellets of enriched uranium—about the size of pencil erasers. The pellets are loaded into thin rods, the rods are tied into bundles of 50 to 300, called fuel assemblies, and anywhere from 100 to 750 fuel assemblies are placed in the reactor core. Here a *controlled* chain reaction (in a bomb the chain reaction is uncontrolled) takes place. It produces the heat to boil water and provide the steam that turns electric turbines.

The rods and assemblies, however, wear away as the U-235 atoms are used up. Each year about one third has to be removed from the reactor core and tossed into a big water storage pool to cool off. It is these *spent* fuel assemblies that are called waste.

This waste contains more than fifty kinds of radioactive isotopes. Some lose their toxic quality in a few hours. Others are dangerous for decades, even centuries. Strontium-90, for instance, is harmful to human beings—especially children and pregnant women—for as long as three hundred years. Plutonium is the worst of all; it is radioactive for tens of thousands of years. Unless isolated from the environment, it can cause innumerable cancers in human beings. In fact, if you could divide a pound of plutonium into 4 billion microscopic pieces and place each one in the nostril of a human being, the resulting cancer epidemic years later would endanger the whole human species.

Obviously, only a terrorist would think of spreading this material around. But scientists have known for a long time that plutonium in the waste of nuclear reactors can serve another purpose. It can be separated from the other waste materials by a technique called "reprocessing." That is much cheaper and less complex than other means of acquiring fuel for nuclear bombs. Large reprocessing plants have not worked out too well in the United States (two had to be closed down because of technical defects, one is still being built), but such plants exist in at least thirteen countries, and they are becoming easier and cheaper to build. India evidently had reprocessed plutonium at its Tombay plant—and used it for the 1974 test.

Unlike uranium-235, plutonium does not have to be enriched. Nine pounds of pure plutonium or seventeen pounds of plutonium extracted from reactor waste can be made into an atomic bomb without further modification. A fair-sized reactor provides 500 pounds of plutonium annually in its waste, enough to manufacture 25 or 30 small nuclear bombs. The nuclear power plants that President Ford agreed to sell Egypt will each be capable of providing 700 pounds of plutonium annually—enough for 41 bombs each.

Understandably, then, the 1974 explosion in India stirred concern and controversy. The controversy was between the West on the one hand and India on the other. Canada, which had supplied many of India's nuclear facilities, complained that there had been a breach of faith. The facilities were to be used for peaceful purposes, not for bombs. The United States echoed these sentiments. India in turn argued that it was simply developing nuclear explosives for such peaceful uses as leveling mountains or digging canals. It wasn't interested in making bombs for war. Most people took this with a grain of salt.

India also stated that the two superpowers had no right to complain. They had agreed to halt the arms race, but hadn't. This was the condition set forth in the 1968 Non-Proliferation Treaty in exchange for the promise by non-nuclear states not to acquire nuclear weapons. Obviously, said India, the United States and the Soviet Union hadn't kept their end of the bargain.

The concern in the United States about the 1974 test in India was over what is called "proliferation." Proliferation means to grow, to increase. American leaders didn't want any more members of the "nuclear club." In fact, they would have been happy if only the United States had been able to make nuclear bombs—if the Soviet Union and the others had never learned the secret. But with the Indian test, there were now six nations that could make these weapons, and there might soon be many more.

President Ford had said that, in addition to the six nations that already had atomic devices, there were twenty others with the technical know-how and the material (plutonium) to make them. By 1985, he predicted, there would be forty nations capable of making them. "A world of many nuclear weapons states," he noted, "could become extremely unstable and dangerous."

The Committee for Economic Development (CED), a prestigious group of business leaders, warned that by the year 2000, "one hundred countries will possess the raw materials and the knowledge necessary to produce nuclear bombs." The amount of plutonium produced as a by-product of nuclear power, it said, "would be equivalent in explosive potential to one million bombs of the size that destroyed Nagasaki."

The business organization cautioned that "nuclear military threats between governments may take on many of the characteristics of terrorist threats—such as the blowing up of a single city or a nuclear reactor by an agent smuggled into enemy territory. It also warned of the possibility of theft of nuclear materials "by revolutionaries, terrorists, criminals, or even armed forces during a civil war or a coup d'etat."

In fact, there already have been a number of instances where nuclear materials have "disappeared." The most sensational was the disappearance of 382 pounds from an enrichment facility in Apollo, Pennsylvania. It is believed to have made its way to Israel. Israel naturally denies it, but the CIA has leaked a number of reports stating that the mideast nation has a fair-sized supply. *Time* magazine (April 12, 1976) reported that Israel possessed a "nuclear arsenal of 13 atomic bombs, assembled, stored, and ready to be dropped on enemy forces from specially equipped Kfir and Phantom fighters or Jericho missiles." The weapons are said to have 20-kiloton yields, somewhat more than the Hiroshima bomb.

On the second day of the Yom Kippur war in 1973, says *Time,* these weapons were assembled and "sent to desert arsenals . . . ready for use." In February 1981, a newsletter published by a well-known London magazine said the Israeli had 200 nuclear weapons and were developing a cruise missile. The Israeli foreign office denied the report.

As of 1977, there were nine nations capable of making nuclear weapons, in addition to the six that had already admitted having them. The nine were Australia, Canada, Israel, Japan, West Germany, Belgium, Taiwan, Italy, and South Africa. Twenty-one others would be able to make nuclear bombs by 1982, according to an article in the *Bulletin of the Atomic Scientists.*

This was worrisome enough. But equally distressing was the fact that not all these nations were dependent on *reprocessed* plutonium. Some were buying enrichment plants to produce bomb-grade uranium. Brazil, for instance, had ordered one from Germany. South Africa was developing a simpler form of enrichment, based on a German method called the Becker Jet Nozzle. There are other techniques, dependent on ultra-centrifuges and lasers, that will soon make enrichment much easier.

Pakistan was building an enrichment plant entirely on its own. One of its scientists had worked in a Dutch nuclear facility, which he left in 1975 armed with all kinds of secrets. Back in Pakistan he quietly helped his government order everything it needed to build the plant and advised how to go about it. Experts believe that Pakistan will have bomb-grade uranium in the early or mid-1980's, and will be able to produce what it calls the "Islamic Bomb" soon thereafter.

President Kennedy once remarked that he was haunted by the possibility of "the President of the United States having to face a world in which fifteen or twenty nations may have these weapons. I regard that as the greatest possible danger."

Fred C. Ikle, director of the Arms Control and Disarmament Agency under President Ford, shared the same fears. This is what he said in a 1975 speech: "Up to this point I've been talking about arms-control matters between ourselves and the Soviet Union. . . . But this relationship may not always pose the greatest danger. The nuclear age—from the very first day—confronted us with a more distant danger—a danger that may make us look back on the present as a safe and easy time by comparison. I refer to the possible risks involved in the inevitable worldwide spread of nuclear technology." In a later talk he warned that "we are basically defenseless against threats of nuclear attack that could come from a great many different sources rather than from one or two principal adversaries."

From 1945 to 1980, there were about 135 "little" wars—such as the 1980 Iraq-Iran war. They took from 30 million to 50 million lives, almost as many as were lost in World War II. Almost all these little wars have been fought by nations that did not possess atomic weaponry. Many experts, however, are worried that when weaker nations *do* acquire nuclear arms, some of the little wars will be transformed into nuclear confrontations. And once the firebreak has been breached, the danger of total nuclear war will become intense.

"Soon the atom will have no secrets for anybody," observes President Muammar Quaddafi of Libya. "Some years ago we could hardly procure a fighter squadron. Tomorrow we will be able to buy an atom bomb and all its parts. The nuclear monopoly is about to be broken."

The second nuclear age also posed three other possibilities for proliferation. One was that advanced nations like Germany, France, Britain, and Japan might decide to build arsenals of their own. So far they have complied with America's wishes—either not to have nuclear weapons at all (like Germany) or just a small stockpile (like France). But the day may come when they decide to take an independent course. It is believed, for instance, that Germany, France, and Britain have pressured the United States to allow them to build cruise missiles. This would change the nuclear picture significantly.

A cruise missile is a choice weapon for proliferation. As noted, it is small—12 to 14 feet long. It flies under radar, so that it is hard to detect. And it is cheap—$1.4 million each. For $1 billion or $2 billion, a nation with the required know-how —like Japan or Germany—could manufacture enough cruise missiles to devastate any nation on earth. It is a possibility that may not be immediate, but it must worry many American and Soviet strategists.

Then there is the danger that American allies may seize United States bombs on their own territory. It is not easy, because the bombs have safety locks and are protected by security forces. But it is not impossible. During the Cyprus crisis of 1974, the Pentagon ordered a carrier of the Sixth Fleet to prepare for landing a Marine detachment to recover warheads in Greece and Turkey. Within the two countries at the time were hundreds of atomic weapons with explosive power equal to millions of tons of TNT. Some were mounted or armed for detonation on Greek and Turkish planes. It would not be easy to recover them if the host country decided to use them for its own purposes.

A third problem, of course, was that of individual terrorists. This is certainly not as serious as other forms of proliferation, especially since it would be impossible for any individual to make an H-bomb—it is much too complicated; the most an individual can do is produce a A-bomb. Still, thousands of lives may be in jeopardy if terrorists begin making atomic (fission) weapons. Few insiders dismiss that possibility—it is fairly certain to happen. Experts say a crude nuclear bomb, less than 1 percent as powerful as the Nagasaki bomb, could kill as many as 2,000 people in a typical suburb, or 50,000 people if detonated under a very large skyscraper. Placed in a football stadium, such a weapon would kill everyone present. In 1976, there were more than 1,500 terrorist bombings in the United States; hundreds were killed and injured. If those terrorists had been able to get their hands on plutonium and make fission bombs, the toll would have been much greater. The United States has not yet witnessed such terrorism, but it is a possibility that authorities ponder seriously.

Taking into account the whole range of possibilities, some prominent Americans grew pessimistic during the 1970's. "Unless the arms race and proliferation of nuclear weapons is stopped soon," said Congressman Pete Stark of California, "the industrialized nations of the world, including the United States, are likely to be destroyed within fifteen years."

A group of influential scientists at a Cambridge [Mass.] Forum in 1975 concluded that "nuclear war in some form is likely before the end of this century. It will probably occur as the direct result of a proliferation of nuclear power and weaponry. The more people who have such weapons, the more probable their use." Among the participants at the forum was

George B. Kistiakowsky, once science adviser to President Eisenhower, and Thomas Schelling, Paul Doty, Richard Garwin, and George Rathjens, all of whom have been advisers either to Presidents or the Departments of State and Defense.

On the other hand, one also began to hear arguments that the nation could survive a *small* nuclear war. George Bush, the future Vice President, was especially firm on that score. Asked by journalist Robert Scheer, "How do you win in a nuclear exchange?" he replied, "You have a survivability of command . . . survivability of industrial potential, protection of a percentage of your citizens, and you have a capability that inflicts more damage on the opposition that it can inflict upon you. That's the way you can have a winner. . . ."

A Congressional study in 1979 concluded that in an all-out nuclear war, 165 million Americans and an almost equal number of Russians would be killed. Survivors, it said, would live at the level of people in the Middle Ages. But the two nations *could* recover from a *limited* conflict. As many as 20 million each would die in the United States and the Soviet Union in such an engagement, but that "could be somewhat less damaging than World War II was to the Soviet Union, and Soviet recovery from that conflict was complete."

The United States, on the other hand, has never suffered so many casualties. "The suffering experienced by the South in the decade after 1860," says the report, "provides the nearest analogy, and a case can be made that these effects took a century to wear off."

One thing was clear: the nuclear problem was becoming ever more complex. No one could be exactly sure where the second nuclear age and proliferation were leading to, but everyone knew the dangers were increasing.

10. THE THIRD NUCLEAR AGE

"THE IMMEDIATE CAUSE OF WORLD WAR III
IS THE PREPARATION FOR IT."
C. Wright Mills

Jimmy Carter, the 39th President of the United States, had a background in nuclear science. After graduating from the Naval Academy he became an aide to Admiral Hyman Rickover, working on the nuclear submarine program. He also took courses on nuclear physics at a college in Schenectady, New York. Carter seemed well qualified to deal with this issue, and he seemed to be sympathetic to the idea of containing—and rolling back—the nuclear-arms race.

In an interview with the *New York Times* during the 1976 election campaign Carter ruled out the "possibility of a limited nuclear war" on the grounds that "once you start using these weapons you are likely to get into an all-out war."

Two months before his inauguration, he expressed the hope that the two superpowers would "freeze present developments" and then reduce "step by step, the quantity . . . of atomic weapons." The goal, he said, should be to decrease "dependence on atomic weapons to zero." Again, in his inaugural address, Carter spoke of the need to work for "zero

111

nuclear weapons." That part of the speech received the biggest ovation of the day.

Carter, like his predecessors, however, seemed to get caught up in the rhetoric of the nuclear race. Instead of stopping it, he got swept along with it. He succumbed to the pressures of hawkish elements who were saying that "the Russians are getting ahead of us"—and who demanded still more weaponry.

Carter's administration therefore was little different from Ford's or Nixon's on nuclear issues. So far as is known, he did not consider using atomic or hydrogen bombs in any foreign-policy crisis. But, on the other hand, there were no cutbacks, no freeze, and no movement toward "zero nuclear weapons."

Carter did complete negotiations with the Soviets for a SALT II treaty—negotiations that were begun under Presidents Ford and Nixon. The new pact, finally initialed in June 1979, allowed each superpower 2,400 missiles and bombers—to be reduced in 1981 to 2,250. At the time the United States had 2,283 and the Soviet Union 2,504—which meant that Moscow would have to get rid of 104 delivery vehicles at once, and another 150 in 1981, when the maximum under the Treaty would be cut to 2,250. The United States was practically unaffected by these figures.

But under SALT II the supply of strategic warheads was permitted to jump by about 4,000 warheads for each side. The American arsenal could go from 9,000 to 13,754; the Soviet from 4,000 to 8,124. And again, there were no restrictions on improvement in accuracy. In effect, the Carter-Brezhnev treaty was an agreement for *joint* escalation.

Even so, Carter was unable to get the treaty approved by the United States Senate. To indicate how significantly public opinion had changed, most antiwar groups (though not all) endorsed the SALT II treaty—on the grounds that if it weren't passed, the nuclear race would speed up even more. A proposed amendment to the treaty by Senator Mark Hatfield of Oregon calling for a "moratorium" on producing and deploying new nuclear weapons received little support.

On the other hand, pro-military forces such as the Committee on the Present Danger made a significant impact on national thinking. This was especially true after the Soviet Union sent troops into Afghanistan in 1979.

The mood of the nation altered appreciably during the Carter years. Many citizens felt frustrated. The United States, they thought, was "being pushed around." While the Soviet Union was gaining influence—in such places as Ethiopia, Angola, Afghanistan, Nicaragua—American influence after Vietnam appeared to be waning.

The frustration, moreover, was fed by still another so-called gap: The CIA, the Pentagon, the White House, and many private groups were saying that there was a spending gap, that the Soviet Union was outspending the United States and would soon be ahead. The nation was told that by 1985 all land-based United States missiles would be vulnerable to Soviet attack. (Submarine-launched missiles, of course, would still be invulnerable, but almost no one was making that point.)

In this political climate, Carter's inaugural call for "zero nuclear weapons" became an unmourned casualty. So did his critique against limited nuclear war. Presidential Directive 59, issued toward the end of the Carter administration, showed a remarkable resemblance to the limited nuclear war policy promoted by Defense Secretary James Schlesinger during the Ford and Nixon administrations.

Something new did surface during Carter's term in office, however. It punctuated the fact that the world may be entering a *third* nuclear age. The first was the age of atomic and hydrogen bombs, missiles and MIRVs, limited to a few nations. The second—the present one—is the age of proliferation, in which from forty to a hundred nations may soon be able to produce nuclear weapons. The third, now gathering momentum, may lead us into the kind of warfare no one ever thought possible —except science-fiction writers.

In February 1978, unexpectedly, Defense Secretary Harold Brown advised Congress that the United States must prepare for a war in space. The statement received scant attention— perhaps because the idea was so bizarre. Virtually no one out- side government had been thinking of space as a battleground. On the contrary, there was a general feeling that space was "off limits."

Back in 1967 the United States and the Soviet Union had signed a treaty prohibiting "the placing in orbit around the Earth of any objects carrying nuclear weapons. . . ." The treaty had been rigorously adhered to by both sides. No nuclear bombs are currently orbiting outer space. Presumably this would protect the world from a space war—more accurately, a war originating in space.

But wars in space can be fought in a different manner—and this is what the strategists on both sides have been considering for some time. Their preparations have gone ahead quietly, secretly; and they have been disguised as purely scientific and civilian activities.

When the Soviet Union launched its first satellite, Sputnik, in October 1957, few people suspected there were any military implications. Later, men and women everywhere were mes- merized as Yuri Gagarin performed the first manned space flight aboard Vostok in April 1961 and Alan Shepard, Jr., fol- lowed aboard a Mercury a month afterwards. Still later, begin- ning in 1968, the public sensed a *Star Wars* quality to flights to the moon by American astronauts and in the unmanned satel- lites probing planets Venus and Mars.

The space program, however, was not as innocuous as originally believed. True, it did promise many civilian benefits: products that could be manufactured in space far better than on earth; the long-term prospects of mining the moon for iron, titanium, aluminum, and other minerals; solar-power plants; and ultimately space colonies in which millions of people would live.

But all the while there was another side to this drama. Of the money spent for "space" in the two decades after Sputnik, the largest share—more than $50 billion—was for space projects with a military purpose. In fact, 60 percent of all United States satellites have been launched to further military goals. So far these military purposes have been *supplemental*––that is, the satellites help the Pentagon take pictures of Soviet military installations, improve navigation, and the like. But development of sophisticated weapons such as the laser ray are far advanced. A 1981 Defense Department report says that "the major payoff" for these space weapons may be only "ten or twenty years away."

Paul C. Warnke, former head of the Arms Control and Disarmament Agency, predicts a space war in the near future. "There is no question in my mind," he told *Business Week* in mid-1979, "that we could have war in space within a decade unless we devise a treaty that will stop it." These sentiments are shared by Malcolm R. Currie, a former high Defense Department official, and many others.

The militarization of space began on earth. In the late 1950's the United States established a supersecret agency to keep track of artificial objects in space. The Space Detection and Tracking System (SPADATS) was assigned the job of tracking all man-made objects up high. As of 1978, it was monitoring 4,000 satellites and gadgets—keeping a record of where they were at a particular moment.

Some, of course, were primarily for commercial purposes—for instance, satellites for transmitting television and radio signals. Others had both a civilian and military purpose, such as weather satellites.

But there were still other satellites directly related to the art of war. Among them were reconnaissance satellites—launched by both powers to see what the other was doing. They are now equipped with cameras so sensitive they can photograph objects 25,000 miles away. In effect, they do what the old human spy or the spy airplane (the U-2) used to do—but more accurately. They count Soviet missile silos, photograph factories, airfields, and anything else of military significance. Flying at 30,000 kilometers an hour, a reconnaissance satellite can take a picture of thousands of square kilometers on a single frame of film.

What was science fiction only a generation ago has now become reality. There are "electronic reconnaissance satellites" to pinpoint the other side's radar systems. There are "ocean surveillance satellites" designed to monitor battleships and shore facilities. There are the navigation satellites, which are indispensable for guiding missiles, aircrafts, and ships to their destination. There are communications satellites, meteorologic (weather) satellites, and geodetic (measuring exact distances on earth) satellites. Most important are the "early warning satellites," which are now so sophisticated that they can advise about an enemy missile launching as soon as it takes place.

Needless to say, if either side could shoot down the other side's early-warning satellites, as well as navigational and communications satellites, the enemy would be vulnerable to a "first strike." He would not know that an attack was coming, or where it was headed. His missile silos, airfields, command posts, and other military installations might be destroyed before he could retaliate. In military jargon this is called a *"disarming* first strike."

It is not surprising that the United States and the Soviet Union have been working on "interceptor"—or "killer"—satellites. As early as 1960, the Air Force was saying that in a few years Moscow could have killer satellites capable of shooting down American early-warning satellites when they became operational in 1963. A United States antisatellite vehicle was therefore designed to counter Soviet interceptors. It was called SAINT—satellite interceptor. Other, imaginative interceptors followed. One interceptor will blind an enemy satellite by spewing it with metal pellets; another by throwing paint on its optical windows. Still another one on the planning boards is a small rocket dispatched from high-flying aircraft, that will zero in on an enemy satellite and kill it.

Since February 1962, a blanket of great secrecy has been thrown around the military satellite program. But details continue to leak out. The program can be divided into three parts:

1. Killer satellites being developed to destroy Soviet satellites.

2. Laser rays, particle beams, and similar weaponry, aimed at "killing" Soviet *missiles* on takeoff.

3. The space shuttle.

The word *laser* stands for light amplification by stimulated emission of radiation. It is a concentrated beam of light that can destroy objects far away, almost instantaneously. Experiments on the laser have been going on since 1960, and at a more rapid pace after 1968. In 1975 a killer laser proved effective in damaging an airplane, and in 1978 in "killing" antitank missiles. Both superpowers have great hopes for it.

In the scenario envisioned by the Pentagon, a killer laser aboard a low-orbit satellite would aim at, and shatter, enemy missiles shortly after being launched—before they could discharge their multiple warheads. According to Senator Malcolm Wallop of Wyoming, just three dozen killer lasers could encompass the whole globe, each capable of firing a thousand "shots." That would be enough to destroy every Soviet missile —and more. In theory, at least, it would be the perfect defense —what the Pentagon has been looking for since 1945.

Like a "disarming first strike" a perfect defense would make it possible to "win" a nuclear war. The United States would be able to save all or most of its population from "damage," whereas the Soviet Union would be entirely vulnerable. It could be destroyed without being able to retaliate.

Of course, the laser may be no more practical than the old antimissile missile (ABM). There are skeptics in the scientific community who insist it won't work, or at least not as well as expected. Richard L. Garwin, a Harvard physicist who has been a consultant to the Pentagon for many years, says that lasers will cost too much and may give the illusion of a perfect defense, when, in fact they aren't.

Garwin, like Warnke, also urges the superpowers to ban killer satellites. "Rather than welcoming the opportunity to turn space into a boxing ring for a series of fights . . ." he says, "we should use our human and material resources more effectively to maintain our security and well-being."

Kosta Tsipis, a prominent New England scientist, considers the laser beam program wasted money on something destined not to work.

The third part of the military space program centers on the space shuttle. Unlike an ordinary satellite shot into the outer reaches, the space shuttle is reusable. It comes back to earth after a voyage in space, and can be relaunched about a hundred times. In that respect it resembles an airplane.

The first space shuttle was 122 feet long and had a capacity for 32 tons of cargo. Hundreds of miles above earth, guided by human pilots, the shuttle is expected to do many feats for private industry. But it will also be able to launch eighteen satellites of the Navastar global positioning system that will make the positioning of American bombers, ships, and missiles far more accurate. It eventually may place satellites in space, and carry laser beams, particle beams, space mines, and the like.

"The country that controls space controls the new era," says Tom Feaster, a high official of the National Aeronautics and Space Administration. "I see space as primarily useful for peaceful purposes. But you are kidding yourself if you don't think it would be useful for defense."

The Air Force claims it is opposed to a space race. "But in the absence of an agreement," it argues, "and in the face of proven Soviet capabilities, the Air Force must work to defend United States satellites, if necessary." Neither side seems able to stop, out of fear the other may catch up to or get ahead of it.

The Soviet Union, of course, is working on the same technology. And it is touch and go which nation will come out first. The technology is mind-boggling—antisatellite vehicles carrying a warhead (nuclear or non-nuclear) that is touched off from the ground; antisatellite weapons fired from fighter planes that "catch" their targets with heat-seeking devices; antisatellite vehicles that are themselves satellites and can be kept in orbit indefinitely; "death rays" of subatomic particles.

If it has an unreal flavor to it, space war nonetheless is being seriously planned. Lieutenant General Daniel O. Graham, who headed the Defense Intelligence Agency until 1975, and was a senior adviser to President Reagan during the 1980 election campaign, is one of the nation's leading enthusiasts for this kind of warfare.

Talking with two *Rolling Stone* writers in September of that year, Graham said it was a mistake to put so much emphasis on "highly expensive . . . offensive missiles like the MX." Instead, he urged that we "use our superiority in space technology to get a space system fast." As he sees it, the United States will be firing either lasers or other weapons from space—and destroying Soviet missiles over the North Pole instead of waiting for them to hit the United States—"which to me is complete idiocy."

"You have to have several space vehicles coming around," he argues, "so that at any given time, you have at least some defense in the right area to pick up an upcoming Soviet threat." Graham was asked if the technology was already available for such combat. "Yes," he replied, "we can practically take it off the shelf."

The Reagan administration evidently was also enthusiastic about the military uses of space. Early in 1981 it was reported that the new regime would ask for an increase in spending for military space programs from $7 billion to $10 billion. Another $500 million would be used for military programs to be performed by the space shuttle.

A book published by a Swedish research agency in 1978 was titled *Outer Space—Battlefield of the Future?*

Will it be? It is beginning to look that way.

11. CATASTROPHE BEYOND CONCEPTION

"TIME IS TWO-EDGED. IT NOT ONLY FORCES US NEARER
TO OUR DOOM IF WE DO NOT SAVE OURSELVES, BUT . . .
IT HABITUATES US TO EXISTING CONDITIONS. . . ."
Bernard Baruch

Sir Solly Zuckerman, a Nobel prize laureate, was Britain's chief science adviser for many years. The best kind of victory, he said, was one in which "the adversary surrenders without a shot being fired." He knows that he cannot win, so he gives up.

That is what great nations have always wanted—to enjoy such overwhelming power that no one dares defy them.

Harry Truman thought the atom bomb gave the United States that power, but it didn't. The Presidents who followed hoped that other technological wonders would make it impossible for any government to challenge the United States. None of them did—not the H-bomb, not the nuclear submarine, not the ballistic missile, not the MIRV, not the MARV.

Each action brought a reaction. In the end, neither side had the capability to deliver a knockout blow.

During the 1980's, however, both sides are still trying. The United States is readying cruise missiles, MX missiles, Trident missiles, and revving up for a space race. The Soviet Union is working on similar projects.

More and more often during the Carter and Reagan administrations political leaders began downplaying the dangers. Nuclear wars, the nation was told by such people as George Bush (the future Vice-President), were "survivable." When an interviewer—Robert Scheer—asked Bush, "Do you mean like 5 percent would survive?" Bush shot back: "More than that—if everybody fired everything he had, you'd have more than that survive." But he wasn't specific.

Such views coming from major American figures indicate that the nuclear race seems destined to continue—until there is a popular revulsion against it. Some people have suggested that Americans will not rise to the danger until there is a terrible accident that kills large numbers of people—something like the near catastrophe in North Carolina in 1961. An accident, or a "small" nuclear war, they say, might galvanize the public against the nuclear race.

Another possibility is that if economic conditions worsen and the government continues to cut back programs for jobs and welfare, the American people may decide they would rather use their tax money for human needs than for armaments.

Perhaps it was popular opposition to President Reagan's economic program—Reaganomics—or simply a growing feeling that "enough is enough." But in late 1981 and early 1982, there was a big swing in the opposite direction on the nuclear issue. A large movement calling for a "freeze" on the testing,

production, and deployment of nuclear weapons suddenly sur-
faced. A few million people signed petitions for a "freeze";
town hall meetings in dozens of New England towns endorsed
the idea; a number of state legislatures approved it; and it
seemed likely that a referendum in California would also urge
a freeze on the national government. In Congress, 170 legisla-
tors, led by Senators Mark Hatfield and Edward Kennedy, introduced a resolution for a "verifiable freeze"; *Time* and *News-
week* made it their lead story that week. Where this new antinu-
clear movement will go remains to be seen.

In any case, there seems to be a race parallel to the military
race. It is a race between those who are hoping—in the words
of Sir Solly Zuckerman—for that one "great" weapon that will
make the United States so superior the Soviets will have to give
up, and those who think the race itself makes nuclear war just
about inevitable.

"The unleashed power of the atom," said Albert Einstein
early in the nuclear age, "has changed everything except our
way of thinking. Thus we are drifting towards a catastrophe
beyond conception."

The nuclear weapon is not just another weapon. For the first
time since human life began on this earth, a war with nuclear
weapons can result in the death of literally everyone.

As Einstein suggested, that's something to think about.

People power will stop nuclear power. The largest demonstration in U.S. history
was held in New York's Central Park on June 12, 1982, in support of nuclear
disarmament.   TRISH PARCELL

CHRONOLOGY

1896 Antoine Henri Becquerel discovers radioactivity.

1902 Marie and Pierre Curie isolate radium.

1905 Albert Einstein formulates the theory of relativity.

1932 James Chadwick discovers the neutron.

1938 Otto Hahn and Fritz Strassman "split" an atom.

1939 Albert Einstein writes letter to Franklin D. Roosevelt urging the United States to undertake a nuclear program. He later says this was his "one great mistake."

1940 British scientists find means to separate U-235 from U-238, a vital link in the production of the bomb.

1942 Enrico Fermi and colleagues produce the first controlled chain reaction in an experiment conducted under the stands of the Alonzo Stagg Stadium at the University of Chicago.

1945 (May) Interim Committee picks four targets for A-bomb in Japan. Secretary of War Henry L. Stimson tells committee that the atomic weapon will represent a new relationship of man to the universe.

1945 (July) First nuclear test. "Fat Man" is exploded at Alamogordo, New Mexico, as top scientists wonder how far the chain reaction will go.

1945 (August) *Enola Gay,* an American airplane, drops the first atomic bomb ever used in warfare on Hiroshima, Japan. Estimates are that 142,000 ultimately died as a result of that raid.

1945 (August) The United States drops a second atomic bomb, this time on the Japanese city of Nagasaki. The drop is one mile off target, but it kills 75,000 people, by present estimates.

1945 (August) Japan surrenders.

1945 (September) Secretary of War Stimson urges an "atomic partnership" with the Soviet Union. Is supported by three other members of the Truman Cabinet, but the President rejects his proposal.

1945 (November) Albert Einstein calls for world government to avoid nuclear war.

1946 Truman gives Soviet Union an ultimatum to evacuate Azerbaijan, a province of Iran, or have the United States unleash atomic bombs on the Soviet Union itself. The Soviets yield.

1946 The Baruch Plan is put before the United Nations. It calls for an international atomic development authority to own and manage everything associated with atomic energy, including the bomb. Soviets reject the plan, because it allows the United States to continue research and production during the interim period.

1946 Secret report prepared for Truman by Clark Clifford urges the United States to prepare to "wage atomic and biological warfare."

1946 Atomic Energy Act is passed. Provides death penalty in peacetime for divulging atomic secrets. It is followed during the Truman and Eisenhower administrations by a host of executive orders to check on the loyalty of federal employees and to classify government documents deemed sensitive.

1949 The Soviet Union detonates its first nuclear device. Within the next fifteen years Great Britain, France, and China also join the nuclear club, detonating their own nuclear devices.

1950 The Korean War begins.

1950 Truman decides to produce the "Super"—the hydrogen bomb—despite unanimous objection by the General Advisory Committee of the Atomic Energy Committee.

1952 "Mike," the first fusion device, is exploded over the Pacific islet Elugelab. Nothing remains of the islet except a hole 175 feet deep and a mile in diameter.

1953 The Soviet Union explodes its first thermonuclear device—nine months after the United States.

1953 Eisenhower threatens to use nuclear weapons if North Korea and China do not come to terms in the Korean War.

1953 Secretary of State John Foster Dulles outlines the administration's nuclear strategy of "massive retaliation" if the Soviet Union crosses beyond its present sphere of influence.

1953 Eisenhower delivers his "atoms for peace" speech to the United Nations, urging use of the atom for "peaceful" purposes such as energy.

1954 United States offers three nuclear weapons to France after its forces are surrounded by the Viet Minh at Dienbienphu.

1954 Bravo, first actual H-bomb, is tested on Bikini, a Pacific atoll. The 15-megaton bomb (equal to 15 million tons of TNT) causes blast damage in an area of 300 square miles and spreads radioactivity over 7,000 square miles.

1954–55 British-French-American disarmament plan is generally accepted by the Soviet Union, but the United States thereupon withdraws its proposal.

1956 Navy establishes a Special Projects Office to develop a solid-fuel rocket that can be launched from a submarine. This is the beginning of America's nuclear submarine program.

1957 Henry Kissinger publishes *Nuclear Weapons and Foreign Policy*, advocating a strategy of limited nuclear war.

1957 First intercontinental ballistic missile, the Atlas, 85 feet long and weighing 120 tons, is launched. It is to be followed by Titan, Minuteman, and MX.

1957 Soviets launch Sputnik, first space vehicle to orbit the earth.

1958 Joint Chiefs of Staff consider use of nuclear weapons in conflict between Formosa and the People's Republic of China over two small islands off the mainland, Quemoy and Matsu.

1958 Petition calling for end of nuclear testing is drafted by Linus Pauling and signed by nine thousand scientists from forty-three countries before being presented to the Secretary General of the United Nations.

1960 During Presidential campaign, candidate John F. Kennedy talks about a "missile gap." Says that by the early 1960's the Soviets will have three times the number of missiles the United States has. In fact, as the Kennedy administration later admitted, there was no such gap; the Soviets had fewer than a hundred missiles.

1961 A few days before leaving office, Eisenhower concedes that talk about a "bomber gap" was "always a fiction."

1961 Kennedy proposes a shelter program to save lives in case of nuclear war, but public fails to respond.

1961 Bay of Pigs invasion. An attempt by 1,400 Cuban exiles, trained by the CIA and accompanied by United States destroyers, to invade Cuba. Cost to the United States is $45 million.

1961 Kennedy administration adopts "graduated response," or "flexible response," strategy. It gives President all options from engaging in CIA activity to small conventional wars to nuclear wars.

1961 Kennedy considers using nuclear weapons against the Communist Pathet Lao if it refuses to participate in a three-sided government in Laos.

1961 Joint Chiefs of Staff formulate plan for using nuclear weapons if the Soviet Union denies access to West Berlin.

1961 B-52 bomber crashes over Goldsboro, North Carolina, releasing two nuclear weapons. One, a 24-megaton bomb, has five of its six safety catches tripped. The one switch that held prevented a major catastrophe. According to government sources, there have been twenty-seven such "broken arrows."

1962 Secretary of Defense Robert S. McNamara outlines "counterforce" strategy at University of Michigan in Ann Arbor. Instead of aiming for the enemy's population centers, the new strategy will focus on his missile silos, airfields, and other military objectives.

1962 October Missile Crisis. The United States and the Soviet Union confront each other directly and come closer to nuclear war than ever before. Crisis ends when the Soviets withdraw the missiles they have secretly placed in Cuba. In return, the United States makes a secret pledge not to allow further attacks on Cuban soil by Cuban exiles, originating from the United States.

1963 The United States and the Soviet Union sign a test-ban treaty prohibiting nuclear tests above ground, but permitting them underground. This loophole allows testing to continue.

1963 Kennedy and Khrushchev approve "hot-line" agreement for direct communication between the leaders of the two countries in case of crisis.

1965–73 Direct United States involvement in the civil war in Vietnam. At the peak of hostilities in 1968, the United States has 542,000 troops on the scene. This is the third most costly war in American history, in terms of casualties suffered.

1968 Non-Proliferation Treaty is signed and later ratified by more than a hundred nations. It is an attempt to stop the spread of nuclear weapons to governments that do not have them, but has not been effective.

1968 General William C. Westmoreland, commander of United States forces in Vietnam, forms a "small secret group" in Saigon to study possible "nuclear defense of Khe Sanh," where American Marines are surrounded.

1968 Presidential candidate Richard M. Nixon secretly warns North Vietnam he will use nuclear weapons against it after he is elected President unless an agreement is readied by November 1969. North Vietnam brushes aside the threat.

1972 The SALT I agreement is signed. It is composed of two parts. The ABM Treaty limits each of the superpowers to two sites for antiballistic missiles. The Interim Agreement sets limits for missiles, nuclear submarines, and bombers.

1973 United States and North Vietnam agree to terms for ending the Vietnam War and for withdrawal of United States troops.

1973 Following failure of Israel to respect a cease-fire in the Yom Kippur war with Egypt, Soviets send ship with nuclear weapons to Alexandria, and United States declares a worldwide Defense Condition 3 (DefCon 3) alert. Nuclear war is avoided when Israeli end hostilities.

1974 India explodes first nuclear device, a 12-kiloton bomb, and becomes sixth member of "nuclear club."

1974 Defense Secretary James Schlesinger announces strategy of "restrained counterforce," a limited nuclear attack against Soviet missile silos, airfields, and command posts, but not cities.

1975 Group of prominent scientists at a Cambridge, Massachusetts, forum state that "nuclear war in some form is likely before the end of this century."

1977 In his inaugural address Jimmy Carter speaks of the need for "zero nuclear weapons"; but in the next four years he increases their number substantially.

1978 Defense Secretary Harold Brown advises Congress that the U.S. "must prepare for a war in space."

1979 United States and Soviet Union initial SALT II agreement, which allows each superpower 2,400 missiles and bombers, to be reduced to 2,250 by 1981. Congress, however, refuses to ratify the agreement.

1979 A Congressional study predicts that in an all-out nuclear war, 165 million Americans and an almost equal number of Russians would be killed.

1980 Carter issues Presidential Directive 59 (PD-59), approving a limited nuclear war strategy against the Soviet Union. It is much like Schlesinger's "restrained counterforce" strategy.

1980 Ronald Reagan's vice-presidential running mate, George Bush, tells journalist Robert Scheer that nuclear wars are "survivable."

1981 Reagan administration announces it will ask for increase in spending for military space programs.

1981 Space shuttle successfully completes first trip into space, marking a new phase of the nuclear age, one in which a war may be fought primarily in space with killer satellites and laser beams.

1982 Negotiations begin in Geneva for limiting intermediate range weapons in Europe, such as the 572 cruise and Pershing missiles the United States plans to place there by 1983, and the SS-20's that the Soviet Union has already positioned.

1981–82 Large antiwar demonstrations take place throughout Europe, involving millions of citizens. The Church plays a prominent role in these demonstrations, especially in The Netherlands.

1982 A new antiwar movement in the United States proposes a "verifiable freeze" of testing, production, and deployment of nuclear weapons and delivery systems. It receives sizeable support in Congress and from the public.

FURTHER READING

Aldridge, Robert C. *The Counterforce Syndrome: A Guide to U.S. Nuclear Weapons and Strategic Doctrine.* Washington, D.C.: Institute for Policy Studies, 1979.

Alperovitz, Gar. *Atomic Diplomacy: Hiroshima and Potsdam.* New York: Simon and Schuster, 1965.

Barnet, Richard J. *The Economy of Death.* New York: Atheneum, 1969.

Berger, John J. *Nuclear Power—The Unviable Option: A Critical Look at Our Energy Alternatives.* Palo Alto, Calif.: Ramparts Press, 1976.

Bernstein, Barton J. and Matusow, Allen J., eds. *The Truman Administration: A Documentary History.* New York: Harper and Row, 1966.

Blackett, Patrick M. *Studies of War: Nuclear and Conventional.* New York: Hill and Wang, 1962.

Brennan, Donald G., ed. *Arms Control, Disarmament and National Security.* New York: George Braziller, 1961.

Carter, Luther. "Political Fallout from Three Mile Island," *Science* (April 13, 1979), pp. 154–155.

Casper, Barry. "Laser Enrichment: A New Path to Proliferation?" *Bulletin of the Atomic Scientists* (January 1977), pp. 28–41.

Cox, John. *Overkill: Weapons of the Nuclear Age.* New York: Thomas Y. Crowell, 1978.

Effects of the possible use of nuclear weapons and the security and economic implications for states of the acquisition and further development of these weapons. United Nations booklet.

Einstein, Albert. *Einstein on Peace.* Otto Nathan and Heinz Norden, eds. New York: Schocken Books, 1960.

Epstein, William. *The Last Chance: Nuclear Proliferation and Arms Control.* New York: Free Press, 1976.

Gyorgy, Anna, et al. *No Nukes: Everyone's Guide to Nuclear Power.* Boston: South End Press, 1979.

Hachiya, Michihiko. *Hiroshima Diary.* Chapel Hill: University of North Carolina Press, 1955.

Hahn, Walter F. and John C. Neff, eds. *American Strategy for the Nuclear Age.* New York: Anchor, 1960.

Halperin, Morton H. *Limited War in the Nuclear Age.* New York: John Wiley and Sons, 1966.

Hersey, John R. *Hiroshima.* New York: Bantam Books, 1948.

Horowitz, David. *From Yalta to Vietnam.* New York: Penguin Books, 1970.

Japan Broadcasting Corporation. *The Unforgettable Fire: Pictures Drawn by Atomic Bomb Survivors.* New York: Pantheon, 1981.

Kahan, Jerome H. *Security in the Nuclear Age: Developing U.S. Strategic Arms Policy.* Washington, D.C.: Brookings Institute, 1975.

Kahn, Herman. *On Thermonuclear War.* New York: Free Press, 1969.

Kennan, George F. *Russia, the Atom, and the West.* New York: Greenwood, 1974.

Kissinger, Henry A. *Nuclear Weapons and Foreign Policy.* New York: Anchor, 1958.

Lapp, Ralph E. *Kill and Overkill.* New York: Basic Books, 1962.

———. *The Voyage of the* Lucky Dragon. New York: Harper, 1958.

———. *The Weapons Culture.* New York: W. W. Norton, 1968.

Laurence, William L. *Men and Atoms: The Discovery, the Uses and the Future of Atomic Energy.* New York: Simon and Schuster, 1961.

Morris, Christopher. *The Day They Lost the H-Bomb.* New York: Coward-McCann, 1966.

Myrdal, Alva. *The Game of Disarmament: How the United States and Russia Run the Arms Race.* New York: Pantheon Books, 1976.

Olson, McKinley C. *Unacceptable Risk: The Nuclear Power Controversy.* New York: Bantam Books, 1976.

Pringle, Laurence. *Nuclear Power: From Physics to Politics.* New York: Macmillan, 1979.

Purcell, John. *Best-Kept Secret: The Story of the Atomic Bomb.* New York: Vanguard Press, 1963.

Sherwin, Martin J. *A World Destroyed: The Atomic Bomb and the Great Alliance.* New York: Alfred A. Knopf, 1975.

Stockholm International Peace Research Institute. *Outer Space: Battlefield of the Future?* New York: Crane, Russak & Co., 1978.

———. *World Armaments and Disarmament.* Cambridge, Mass.: MIT Press (available yearly).

York, Herbert, collated by. *Arms Control,* articles from *Scientific American.* San Francisco: W. H. Freeman, 1973.

INDEX

134

ABOUT THE AUTHOR

SIDNEY LENS is the author of nineteen books on foreign affairs, labor, communism and the American left. A senior editor of *The Progressive* magazine, his articles have appeared in numerous newspapers and magazines, including *Harper's, New Republic, The Nation, The Rotarian, Harvard Business Review,* and *Commonweal.*

Mr. Lens, a long-time union official, was one of the founders of the peace movement, co-chairing the New Mobilization Committee to End the War in Vietnam. He continues to be involved in efforts toward world peace and nuclear disarmament.

Sidney Lens and his wife live in Chicago, Illinois.